Wicked Cupcakes!
LUISA ZISSMAN

Wicked Cupcakes!
LUISA ZISSMAN

TRANSWORLD PUBLISHERS
61–63 Uxbridge Road, London W5 5SA
A Random House Group Company
www.transworldbooks.co.uk

First published in Great Britain
in 2014 by Bantam Press
an imprint of Transworld Publishers

A CIP catalogue record for this book
is available from the British Library.

ISBN 9780593073759

Addresses for Random House Group Ltd companies outside the UK
can be found at: www.randomhouse.co.uk
The Random House Group Ltd Reg. No. 954009

The Random House Group Limited supports the Forest Stewardship Council® (FSC®), the leading international forest-certification organisation. Our books carrying the FSC label are printed on FSC®-certified paper. FSC is the only forest-certification scheme supported by the leading environmental organisations, including Greenpeace. Our paper procurement policy can be found at www.randomhouse.co.uk/environment

Photography: Robin Matthews Photography

Printed and bound in Germany
2 4 6 8 10 9 7 5 3 1

For Dixie, my beautiful princess, who inspires and motivates me every day. My wonderful parents who support me continually and A... I love you all very much xx

CONTENTS

Introduction **8**

Luisa's Guide to Making Perfect Cakes **10**

Luisa's Guide to Funky Cake Decoration **18**

Luisa's Signature Cakes **29**

Girls' Night In **43**

Naughty Cupcakes **57**

Picnic in the Park Cakes **67**

Vintage Cupcakes **79**

Baking with Dixie **89**

Skinny Minnie Cupcakes **109**

Quirky Cupcakes **121**

Index **141**

INTRODUCTION

Writing this book is something of a dream come true for me. Ever since I was little I've been creative – and I've always loved cake – so what better project to sink my teeth into? If you'll pardon the pun...

People always ask if I made cakes with my mum while I was growing up, but as a child I remember spending my days baking with my Italian grandmother. We'd make pizza, bread, Christmas cake – there was always a Christmas cake! And she'd let me help out with making the little models on top, too. Looking back, I think that's where it all began for me – Nonna ignited in me a real passion for baking at a young age.

I really didn't think anything would come of it when I started baking from home, making wacky birthday cakes for friends, but it kind of snowballed and word spread and here I am today, with my own little baking empire!

I started Dixie's Cupcakery in St Albans three years ago. My aim was to provide people with luxury cakes and cupcakes with innovative flavours that they wouldn't normally make or buy. I closed the shop and relocated to bigger premises to focus solely on orders because the main focus of Dixie's was creating cakes and cupcakes for bespoke orders. Dixie loves baking with me and helping create wonderful treats. She may be young, but she actually makes a really good shortbread. I think it's because she's got such little fingers and it all crumbles so well – she could definitely be my secret weapon!

As you'll see when you work your way through the book, I love the decorative side of baking, but I'm also quite experimental – I think of really out-there ideas and then just see if it works. If it doesn't work for you, don't be disheartened – just try again!

When it came to deciding which recipes to put in the book, I selected things that are popular in the shop and a little bit different. I'm not a very measured baker and that's reflected in the book, too – it's very much do this, add a bit of that, stick that in. People might think I'm crazy but, after a few trials and errors, it usually comes out well. We create fun flavours – my Pimm's cake with cucumber icing is a real summer hit – and I think baking should be fun. I don't want to be traditional, so roll up those sleeves and get stuck in!

People always ask about my idols and who I look up to in the industry and that's where the inspiration for this cookbook came from – I really don't think there's anyone young and fun who the under-40s can look up to in the baking world, so I guess I'd like that person to be me. I want to tap into a different generation of bakers and introduce you to a fun new way of baking, vamping it up, making baking sexy and a bit different. There are so many baking books out there and I wanted something that was going to stand out. It's a very pink, very sparkly, very girlie take on baking, with loads of crazy stuff as well as an introduction to basic sugarcraft and decorations, with lots of different recipes, and I really hope you all enjoy it.

I've been credited with making baking sexy and, while that really wasn't a deliberate move of mine, there's nothing wrong with sexing-up baking – I'm young, I look the way I do, I dress a certain way and I go out with my friends. Baking is fashionable and fun and I want to set an example to a new generation of bakers, girls like me.

People keep asking what's next after the book and whether I'm going to have my own baking show. Obviously *The Apprentice* and *Celebrity Big Brother* opened a lot of doors for me and were life-changing, career-boosting experiences.

Before The Apprentice, I owned Dixie's and The Baker Shop – my online business which sells brands such as Wilton and PME. I'm thinking of new ideas, new flavours, new wacky schemes all the time. The Baker Shop, for example, came out of Dixie's – we used to buy packaging to put our cupcakes in, but we're very American in our style at Dixie's, very over the top, and I couldn't find a box tall enough to put the cakes in. So I designed my own, had them manufactured, and eventually started selling them. That's how Bakers Toolkit came about – I was dealing with different suppliers and realized that the industry really isn't that forward-thinking, so I started my own brand tailored to the consumer. No one out there does it exactly how I want it done, so I just think, oh, I'll do my own thing. And that's something I want to encourage you to do when it comes to your own baking.

With this book, I hope you'll learn some new tips and tricks – and of course make some delicious teatime treats. But, more than that, I hope I inspire you to try new recipes, experiment with ideas of your own and really have fun with your baking. After all, if it doesn't turn out quite right, you can just lick the bowl and start again!

Luisa's Guide to
MAKING PERFECT CAKES

The Mix

1 First, take your time – when I rush, it never comes out well. I love getting all my bowls out and measuring all the ingredients first.

2 Put all the dry ingredients – flour, baking powder, cocoa powder, etc. – into the mixer together with the butter and mix until it resembles fine breadcrumbs. It's definitely worth investing in a good mixer, as these help with the consistency of your cakes, making them really light and fluffy – and they take away a lot of the hard work for you, too!

3 While that's mixing, measure out your wet ingredients – eggs, milk and flavourings – and slowly add them to the breadcrumb mixture. I only use free-range eggs, medium size, and ensure they're at room temperature before I start baking. If your eggs are too cold, the cakes won't bake as well – they won't be as light.

4 The secret to making the perfect cake mix is to ensure you combine your ingredients properly. A lot of people only mix for a few minutes. I don't think that's good enough, you really need to mix it well. We do ours in the mixer for 5–10 minutes.

5 Generally, we'll bake cakes for a longer time at a lower temperature to make sure they're evenly cooked. For instance, we'll bake cupcakes at 160°C for 20 minutes as opposed to 180°C for 18 minutes – I find this works better. It is essential, however, to ensure that the oven is at the correct temperature before you put the cakes in.

Removing the seeds from a vanilla pod

Flavourings

1 The usual time to flavour your cakes is when you add your wet ingredients. If you're making vanilla cupcakes, don't use vanilla essence. Opt for vanilla bean paste or extract, or use vanilla pods and scrape the seeds into the batter – I think it makes a real difference to the flavour of the cakes. Add the vanilla along with the eggs and mix well.

2 If you're anything like me, flavouring can sometimes be pretty much trial and error. Just experiment. If you like the flavour of something you can put it into a cake. In the shop, we tend to have a staple cake mix to which we add things. If we're making the Marmite and chocolate cupcakes, for instance, we'll make a basic chocolate cake mixture, then dilute the Marmite in hot water and add that when we add the eggs.

3 When it comes to flavouring cakes, use things you wouldn't normally use – I make a standard cake batter and put a load of rum in it. People ask: 'Well, doesn't that make it really runny?' But just add some more flour and see how it comes out.

4 Cinnamon is a great spice to add to cakes and, generally speaking, if you're adding a dry ingredient, you should add it with the other dry ingredients – so add the cinnamon at the butter/ flour breadcrumb stage.

Lining Tins

Although on the whole we're not dealing with bigger cakes in this book, I wanted to include this bit of general baking advice.

1 If you're making a large cake, find the right size of cake tin for your mixture – too small and the cake will be undercooked, too big and it'll be dry. We use seamless tins in our shop – the springform ones are great and make it easy to extract the cake. But you need to grease and line them well. If you are using muffin trays to make cupcakes, buy the best you can afford – the cheaper ones don't cook the cupcakes evenly. You don't need to grease and line muffin trays – use muffin cases. Bakers Toolkit have a range of high-quality cases that I always use.

2 To grease your cake tin, bring some unsalted butter to room temperature and rub it around the inside of the tin with a piece of kitchen roll, so you can see a buttery sheen. You can buy ready-cut circles of baking parchment in different sizes, but for a cheaper option you can make them yourself. Place your tin on top of some unrolled baking parchment. Take a pencil and draw around the outside edge of the tin, then cut out the shape and place it on the bottom of the greased tin. You could also use cake release – a fantastic product that greases and flours your tin in one. Your cake will come out of the tin perfectly when cooked.

3 With some larger cakes, when they're midway through cooking, after cooling we cover the top with baking parchment too. So it's a good idea to cut another circle the same size as the first before putting the mixture into the tin – just in case it's needed.

4 The cake tin is now ready for the mixture, so pour it in straight away, making sure you use a spatula to get it all out of the bowl. Then smooth it over to create a nice flat top before placing it in the oven.

How to Deal with Disasters

- If your muffin cases peel away from the side of your cupcakes on cooling, it means your mixture is too wet – next time, add more flour. You also need to use good-quality muffin cases, the really thick ones, and this will help stop it happening too.

- A cracked cupcake isn't necessarily a disaster – icing can hide the ugliest of sins, and the perfect cupcake will have icing piled high. To avoid those open tops, though, learn to judge whether your cake batter's too dry or not. A batter without enough moisture can erupt when it's baked, so learn to add a little water and thin the batter down – it should be like thick custard.

- Sunken cakes are almost always the result of a baker not having enough willpower! Nobody's more guilty of this than me – but, no matter how tempting the cakes smell, you have to resist the temptation to open the oven door. Opening the oven will lower the temperature, and that's what causes cakes to sink. Instead, only open the oven door once you're fairly certain they're done – if you're making a large cake, a skewer inserted into the centre should come out clean, with no cake batter on it. If you're making cupcakes, press them gently – they should be firm and spring back to your touch. Once out of the oven, cool your cakes on a wire rack away from open windows and doors, where sudden temperature changes could still cause them to sink. Luckily, a sunken cake tastes just as good as a perfectly-shaped one, so don't worry too much!

- We've all been there – the cakes look gorgeous, but the heart of the bake is too damp and doughy; the outside's cooked, but the inside's still raw. This is almost always an indication that the mixture was too wet to begin with – or that the cakes were baked at too high a heat. Next time, make sure the batter has a perfect Goldilocks consistency – not too wet, not too dry – and try adding a little more liquid or flour until you get it to the perfect state.

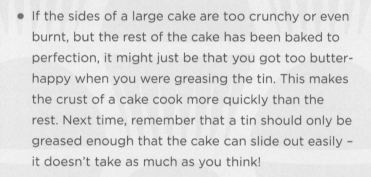

- If the sides of a large cake are too crunchy or even burnt, but the rest of the cake has been baked to perfection, it might just be that you got too butter-happy when you were greasing the tin. This makes the crust of a cake cook more quickly than the rest. Next time, remember that a tin should only be greased enough that the cake can slide out easily – it doesn't take as much as you think!

- If your icing just won't stay put, chances are there's too much liquid in the mix. Stir in a little more icing sugar – or cocoa powder, if you're making a chocolate icing – and the mixture will soon thicken. And remember to always let your cakes cool down before you begin icing – much as you might want to eat your crazy creations immediately, the heat from the cakes will melt the icing and it won't keep its shape. If your kitchen's particularly warm, it can often help to refrigerate your icing for a little while before beginning your decorations.

Luisa's Guide to
FUNKY CAKE
DECORATION

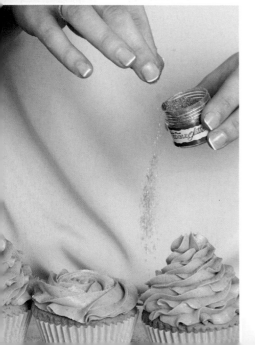

Buttercream

Buttercream is my favourite kind of icing – it tastes so nice and looks so pretty. My top tip is to use a disposable icing bag – it's so much easier than washing up!

1 A lot of people say they can't get their buttercream right. I always use the standard two parts icing sugar to one part butter, so if you have 1kg of icing sugar, use 500g of unsalted butter and add a splash of milk. Put it all in a mixer and whip it – we whip our icing for 10–15 minutes on a high speed.

2 Here's a cheap and easy tip for not getting icing sugar all over the kitchen. Dampen a tea towel and put it over your basin – it stops it going everywhere.

3 When flavouring buttercreams, try to use fresh flavourings – fresh lime zest in plain buttercream or a touch of Baileys in chocolate buttercream are amazing. If you're adding a dry ingredient, you'll need to balance it out with a touch more liquid (i.e. milk). If you're using a wet flavouring, replace some of the milk with it so that you get the consistency right. Too runny and the icing won't hold its shape when piped, too dry and it won't come out of the icing bag without a struggle.

4 Now fill the icing bag. To start, cut the bottom of your bag to create a hole big enough for a star nozzle and insert the nozzle into the hole, being careful not to nick the bag on the way down or all the icing will squirt out as you pipe. Spoon your buttercream into the bag and clamp it at the top with a food clip to prevent it spilling out. Now you're ready to pipe.

5 Always squeeze only from the top of the bag, using the hand you write with. Your spare hand should only hold the middle for support, to keep the bag upright – if you hold your bag at an angle, your icing will be wonky. Start piping from the outside and go round the cupcake one, two, three times, overlapping the previous row of piping slightly as you go. Finish it off with a full stop motion at the top, so you get that perfect finish, a kind of buttercream mountain look (see p 22).

6 To pipe roses, use the rose tip nozzle – it's like the star nozzle but more closed. For these, you start from the inside and pipe out. I tend to pipe in the middle of the cupcake for 3–5 seconds to make a bud, then move out, keeping the icing flat. Move the nozzle in a round motion and as you do so make your circle wider. Make sure you keep the nozzle close to the previous piece of piping and you'll get a perfect rose (see p 23). I think it's the easiest one to do.

7 To use a palette knife to apply your icing, get a scoop of icing and pile it into the middle of your cupcake. Using the back of your palette knife, scrape down so that you form a dome shape on the cupcake. Then, still using the back of your knife, scoop round so you get a smooth, domed finish.

8 For a quick and easy finish, sprinkle some edible glitter over your iced cupcakes – I think it looks amazing. I put glitter on everything – it's like a little dusting of love! Or, if you're making cocktail cupcakes, for a mojito for instance, decorate with fresh mint and some sugar sand – it's a really good effect and so easy to do too. We stick things such as straws, umbrellas and those plastic cocktail stirrers into our cocktail cupcakes – although obviously you'll take all these out before you eat them!

Hand-made Decorations

We don't buy pre-made decorations at Dixie's, we use different cutters with ready-to-roll icing and we hand-model our figures. If we're making specific flowers, we'll use flower paste or Mexican modelling paste, as it holds delicate shapes better. For edible pastes, glue and glitter, see www.the-bakershop.co.uk.

1 Take a flat baking sheet and place a sheet of baking parchment on top – this will stop the decorations sticking to the sheet as they dry.

2 Take a ball of ready-to-roll fondant icing and add a teaspoon of CMC powder to it – it's a hardening agent that will enable your decorations to harden as they dry (if you have time to make your decorations the day before, they will harden naturally and you won't need it). Then dust your surface with icing sugar and roll ithe icing out to around 5mm thick.

3 Next, take your chosen cutter and push it down into the icing. Lift the cutter – if the decoration stays on the surface, carefully remove it with a palette knife; if it stays in the cutter, remove it gently with your finger – then place on the baking parchment. Do this until you have enough decorations (make a couple extra in case of breakages) and leave to air-dry overnight.

4 The following day, it's time to make your decorations look even prettier. If you've made flowers, roll a small piece of yellow ready-to-roll icing into a ball and attach that to the centre of the flower. Or paint the tips of the flowers with edible glue and dip them into some edible glitter – this creates a really pretty look and it's so simple. The decorations will keep in an airtight container, once completely dry, for about a month.

5 When it comes to using your decorations, if you are putting them on cupcakes, put them in place while the buttercream is still wet. If you're putting them on to a fondant-iced cake, use a small dab of edible glue to stick them in place.

LUISA'S
SIGNATURE CAKES

The cakes in this chapter are inspired by the classic recipes from my shop, Dixie's Cupcakery, where my baking dreams began, with all the classic favourite cakes - chocolate, cookies and cream and cheesecake cupcakes heavily laden with fresh berries. These are the perfect cupcakes to serve at any time of day.

INDULGENT CHOCOLATE CUPCAKES

These cakes are rich, indulgent and delicious and are probably our top seller at the bakery. I don't know anyone who doesn't like a good chocolate cupcake. The best thing about these cakes is that you can easily pimp the flavour with the addition of orange or mint.

Preheat the oven to 160°C/325°F/Gas Mark 3.

Using a mixer, whisk together the butter, caster sugar and light brown sugar until light and creamy. Add the eggs and whisk again. Gently fold in the flour, cocoa powder, bicarbonate of soda, soured cream, vanilla bean paste and salt, using a spatula.

To pimp the cakes, you can add different flavourings to the batter and decorate them to match. For instance, add the zest of 2 oranges and 200g of chopped orange chocolate to the batter, or add 2 teaspoons of peppermint essence to the batter, along with 200g of chopped mint-flavoured chocolate.

Divide the cake mixture between the muffin cases and bake for 20 minutes, until the cakes are firm to touch and a skewer inserted into the centre of one of them comes out clean, with no cake batter on it. Transfer to a rack to cool.

For the buttercream, whisk together the icing sugar, cocoa powder, butter and milk to make a rich chocolate frosting. Spoon into the piping bag and pipe a swirl on top of the cooled cupcakes.

Add decorations to match the flavour of your cakes: for example, orange pieces for chocolate orange cupcakes, or mint leaves for mint choc cupcakes.

The cakes will keep for up to 3 days if stored in an airtight container.

PREPARATION TIME: 30 MINUTES
BAKING TIME: 20 MINUTES
MAKES 12 CAKES

FOR THE CAKE MIXTURE
100G UNSALTED BUTTER, SOFTENED
100G CASTER SUGAR
100G LIGHT BROWN SUGAR
4 EGGS
160G SELF-RAISING FLOUR, SIFTED
60G COCOA POWDER, SIFTED
1 TEASPOON BICARBONATE OF SODA
80ML SOURED CREAM
2 TEASPOONS VANILLA BEAN PASTE
A PINCH OF SALT

FOR CAKE FLAVOURINGS (OPTIONAL)
ZEST OF 2 ORANGES AND 200G ORANGE CHOCOLATE, CHOPPED, OR
2 TEASPOONS PEPPERMINT ESSENCE AND 200G OF MINT CHOCOLATE, CHOPPED

FOR THE BUTTERCREAM
300G ICING SUGAR, SIFTED
40G COCOA POWDER, SIFTED
150G UNSALTED BUTTER, SOFTENED
60ML MILK

TO DECORATE
ORANGE SEGMENTS, OR
FRESH MINT LEAVES

EQUIPMENT: MIXER, 12-HOLE MUFFIN TIN LINED WITH MUFFIN CASES, PIPING BAG FITTED WITH LARGE STAR NOZZLE

COOKIES AND CREAM CUPCAKES

Whether you like to dunk yours in milk, lick off the filling or just munch them, Oreo cookies are a surefire winner in my book. These cupcakes have a secret Oreo cookie base that softens as they are cooked. Kids just love it when they find the hidden cookie in the cupcake.

PREPARATION TIME: 25 MINUTES

BAKING TIME: 20 MINUTES

MAKES 12 CAKES

FOR THE CUPCAKES

12 REGULAR-SIZED CREME-FILLED
   CHOCOLATE COOKIES, SUCH AS OREOS

200G UNSALTED BUTTER, SOFTENED

220G CASTER SUGAR

4 EGGS

220G SELF-RAISING FLOUR, SIFTED

2 TEASPOONS BAKING POWDER

2 TEASPOONS VANILLA BEAN PASTE OR
VANILLA EXTRACT

FOR THE BUTTERCREAM

300G ICING SUGAR, SIFTED

150G UNSALTED BUTTER, SOFTENED

1–2 TABLESPOONS WHOLE MILK

FINELY CRUSHED CREME-FILLED
   CHOCOLATE COOKIES, SUCH AS OREOS

TO DECORATE

36 MINI CREME-FILLED CHOCOLATE
   COOKIES, SUCH AS OREOS

**EQUIPMENT: MIXER, 12-HOLE MUFFIN TIN
LINED WITH MUFFIN CASES, PIPING BAG
FITTED WITH LARGE STAR NOZZLE**

Preheat the oven to 160°C/325°F/Gas Mark 3.

Place a whole cookie in the base of each muffin case. Using a mixer, whisk together the butter and caster sugar until light and creamy. Add the eggs and whisk again. Gently fold in the flour, baking powder and vanilla bean paste, using a spatula.

Spoon the cake mixture over the cookies so that they are completely covered. Bake for 20 minutes, until the cakes are firm to touch and a skewer inserted into the centre of one of them comes out clean, with no cake batter on it. Transfer to a rack to cool.

For the buttercream, whisk together the icing sugar, butter, crushed cookies and enough milk to make a smooth, stiff frosting. Spoon it into the piping bag and pipe a swirl on to each cake and place a whole mini cookie on top of each cake.

The cakes will keep for up to 3 days if stored in an airtight container.

CHEESECAKE CUPCAKES

Cheesecake is such a popular dessert and makes a perfect cupcake with a buttery biscuit base. I like them best as plain vanilla, but you can top these cheesecakes with fresh berries and a drizzle of berry sauce and serve them for dessert if you wish.

Preheat the oven to 160°C/325°F/Gas Mark 3.

In a food processor, blitz the digestive biscuits to fine crumbs. Stir in the melted butter and mix well until all the crumbs are coated. Divide the crumbs between the muffin cases and press down with the back of a spoon to compact the crumbs into a layer.

Using a mixer, whisk together the butter and caster sugar until light and creamy. Add the eggs and whisk again. Gently fold in the flour and baking powder, using a spatula.

For the cream cheese filling, whisk together the cream cheese, egg and caster sugar in a separate bowl. It is best to have the cream cheese at room temperature when you do this, otherwise the filling can be lumpy.

Place a spoonful of the cake mixture in each muffin case on top of the biscuit base, then top with a layer of cream cheese filling and finish with a further spoonful of cake batter so that the cheesecake filling is covered.

Bake in the oven for 20 minutes, until the cakes are firm to touch and spring back when you press them with your fingertips. Remove from the oven and leave to cool.

To make the icing, whisk together the icing sugar, butter and cream cheese in a mixing bowl until light and creamy. Spoon into the piping bag and pipe a swirl on top of the cooled cupcakes. Top with fresh berries and a drizzle of strawberry sauce just before serving.

These cakes will keep for up to 3 days if stored in the refrigerator.

PREPARATION TIME: 30 MINUTES
BAKING TIME: 20 MINUTES
MAKES 12 CAKES

FOR THE BISCUIT BASE
120G DIGESTIVE BISCUITS
60G UNSALTED BUTTER, MELTED

FOR THE CUPCAKE SPONGES
100G UNSALTED BUTTER, SOFTENED
110G CASTER SUGAR
2 EGGS
110G SELF-RAISING FLOUR
2 TEASPOONS BAKING POWDER

FOR THE CREAM CHEESE FILLING
200G CREAM CHEESE
1 EGG
75G CASTER SUGAR

FOR THE CREAM CHEESE ICING
450G ICING SUGAR, SIFTED
70G UNSALTED BUTTER, SOFTENED
180G CREAM CHEESE

TO DECORATE
FRESH BERRIES
STRAWBERRY ICE-CREAM TOPPING

EQUIPMENT: FOOD PROCESSOR, MIXER, 12-HOLE MUFFIN TIN LINED WITH 6 MUFFIN CASES, PIPING BAG FITTED WITH LARGE STAR NOZZLE

CHOCOLATE PEANUT BUTTER FUDGE CUPCAKES

These are one of Dixie Cupcakery's most indulgent cakes – peanut chocolate sponge, topped with peanut butter frosting, chopped honey-coated peanuts and mini Reese's Peanut Butter Cups. They are one of my favourites!

PREPARATION TIME: 25 MINUTES
BAKING TIME: 20 MINUTES
MAKES 12 CAKES

FOR THE CUPCAKES
100G UNSALTED BUTTER, SOFTENED
100G CASTER SUGAR
100G LIGHT BROWN SUGAR
4 EGGS
160G SELF-RAISING FLOUR, SIFTED
60G COCOA POWDER, SIFTED
1 TEASPOON BICARBONATE OF SODA
80ML SOURED CREAM
4 TABLESPOONS CRUNCHY PEANUT
   BUTTER
A PINCH OF SALT

FOR THE BUTTERCREAM
300G ICING SUGAR, SIFTED
150G UNSALTED BUTTER, SOFTENED
2 TABLESPOONS SMOOTH PEANUT BUTTER
60ML MILK

TO DECORATE
HONEY-ROASTED PEANUTS, FINELY
   CHOPPED
MINI REESE'S PEANUT BUTTER CUPS
   (OPTIONAL)

EQUIPMENT: MIXER, 12-HOLE MUFFIN TIN
LINED WITH MUFFIN CASES, PIPING BAG
FITTED WITH LARGE STAR NOZZLE

Preheat the oven to 160°C/325°F/Gas Mark 3.

Using a mixer, whisk together the butter, caster sugar and light brown sugar until light and creamy. Add the eggs and whisk again. Gently fold in the flour, cocoa powder, bicarbonate of soda, soured cream, peanut butter and salt, using a spatula.

Divide the mixture between the muffin cases and bake for 20 minutes, until the cakes are firm to touch and a skewer inserted into the centre of one of them comes out clean, with no cake batter on it. Transfer to a rack to cool.

For the buttercream, whisk together the icing sugar, butter, peanut butter and enough milk to make a smooth, stiff frosting. Spoon it into the piping bag and pipe a swirl on to each cake. Sprinkle with the chopped peanuts and decorate with the mini Peanut Butter Cups.

These cakes will keep for up to 3 days in an airtight container.

APPLE CRUMBLE CUPCAKES

Apple crumble was one of the first things I learnt to bake when I was a kid. It is still a popular dessert in my house today, and it's the inspiration for these warming spiced cupcakes. With apple batter, flavoured with cinnamon and nutmeg, cinnamon frosting and buttery crumble topping, these are great cupcakes to serve to friends and family. If you like, you can serve them as a dessert, with hot golden custard on the side.

PREPARATION TIME: 25 MINUTES

BAKING TIME: 25-30 MINUTES

MAKES 12 CAKES

FOR THE CUPCAKES

200G UNSALTED BUTTER, SOFTENED

220G DARK BROWN SUGAR

4 EGGS

220G SELF-RAISING FLOUR, SIFTED

3 TEASPOONS BAKING POWDER

2 TEASPOONS VANILLA BEAN PASTE OR
   VANILLA EXTRACT

A PINCH OF FRESHLY GRATED NUTMEG

2 TEASPOONS GROUND CINNAMON

4 COOKING APPLES, PEELED, CORED AND
   FINELY DICED

FOR THE BUTTERCREAM

300G ICING SUGAR, SIFTED

1 TABLESPOON DARK BROWN SUGAR

1 TEASPOON GROUND CINNAMON

150G UNSALTED BUTTER, SOFTENED

1-2 TABLESPOONS WHOLE MILK

FOR THE CRUMBLE TOPPING

1 TABLESPOON BUTTER, SOFTENED

1 TABLESPOON BROWN SUGAR

2 TABLESPOONS PLAIN FLOUR

½ TEASPOON GROUND CINNAMON

A PINCH OF FRESHLY GRATED NUTMEG

**EQUIPMENT: GREASED AND LINED BAKING
TRAY, MIXER, 12-HOLE MUFFIN TIN LINED
WITH MUFFIN CASES**

Preheat the oven to 160°C/325°F/Gas Mark 3.

Begin by preparing the crumble. Place the butter, sugar, flour, cinnamon and nutmeg in a bowl and rub together with clean fingertips to form large crumbs. Sprinkle on the prepared baking tray in a thin layer and bake in the oven for 5–10 minutes, until the crumbs start to turn golden brown. Remove from the oven and leave to cool on the tray. Leave the oven on.

Using a mixer, whisk together the butter and brown sugar until light and creamy. Add the eggs and whisk again. Gently fold in the flour, baking powder, vanilla bean paste, nutmeg and cinnamon, using a spatula. Add the apple pieces and stir again so that they are all coated in the batter. (If you chop the apples ahead of time, coat them with a little lemon juice to prevent them discolouring.)

Divide the mixture between the muffin cases and bake for 20 minutes, until the cakes are firm to touch and a skewer inserted into the centre of one of them comes out clean, with no cake batter on it. Transfer to a rack to cool.

For the buttercream, whisk together the icing sugar, dark brown sugar, cinnamon, butter and enough milk to make a smooth, stiff frosting. Spread it over the top of each cake with a palette knife and sprinkle with the cooled crumble mixture.

These cakes will keep for up to 3 days in an airtight container and are delicious served warm with custard.

SALTED CARAMEL CUPCAKES

Toffee cakes with a hollowed-out cavity filled with salted caramel sauce and topped with salted caramel butter cream and shards make an indulgent treat.

PREPARATION TIME: 25 MINUTES
BAKING TIME: 20 MINUTES
MAKES 12 CAKES

FOR THE CUPCAKES
200G UNSALTED BUTTER, SOFTENED
220G CASTER SUGAR
4 EGGS
220G SELF-RAISING FLOUR, SIFTED
2 TEASPOONS BAKING POWDER
4 TABLESPOONS DOLCE DE LECHE
  CARAMEL SAUCE
1 TEASPOON SEA SALT FLAKES

FOR THE FILLING
6 TABLESPOONS DOLCE DE LECHE
  CARAMEL SAUCE

FOR THE BUTTERCREAM
300G ICING SUGAR, SIFTED
150G UNSALTED BUTTER, SOFTENED
2 TABLESPOONS DOLCE DE LECHE
  CARAMEL SAUCE
½ TEASPOON SEA SALT FLAKES
1–2 TABLESPOONS WHOLE MILK

FOR THE CARAMEL SHARDS
100G CASTER SUGAR

EQUIPMENT: MIXER, 12-HOLE MUFFIN TIN
LINED WITH MUFFIN CASES, CUPCAKE
PLUNGER OR SHARP KNIFE, BAKING TRAY
LINED WITH BAKING PAPER, PIPING BAG
FITTED WITH LARGE STAR NOZZLE

Preheat the oven to 160°C/325°F/Gas Mark 3.

Using a mixer, whisk together the butter and caster sugar until light and creamy. Add the eggs and whisk again. Gently fold in the flour, baking powder, caramel sauce and salt, using a spatula.

Divide the mixture beween the muffin cases and bake for 20 minutes, until the cakes are firm to touch and a skewer inserted into the centre of one of them comes out clean, with no cake batter on it. Transfer to a rack to cool.

When the cakes are cool, remove the centre of each cupcake using a cupcake plunger or a sharp knife, and fill the hole with a little caramel sauce. Replace the removed cake on top of the caramel.

For the buttercream, whisk together the icing sugar, butter, caramel sauce, salt and enough milk to make a smooth, stiff frosting. Spoon into the piping bag and pipe a swirl on top of each cake.

For the caramel shards, heat the sugar in a pan until it melts and starts to turn golden brown. Do not stir the sugar, but swirl the saucepan over the heat from time to time to ensure even cooking. Watch carefully – when the sugar melts, it can easily burn. When melted, pour the caramel on to the prepared baking tray, either in one large piece or swirling the melted sugar into pretty patterns. Leave to set for about 20 minutes, until the caramel is cool. If you have made a large sheet of caramel, break it into shards. Decorate the tops of the cupcakes with the sugar shards or patterned decorations and serve straight away. The sugar decorations need to be made shortly before serving, as they become sticky over time when exposed to air.

GIRLS' NIGHT IN

Like the best of you, I love to go out on the town, but sometimes the most enjoyable nights for me are those spent at home with a group of my girlfriends, having fun and pampering ourselves. This chapter contains perfectly naughty cakes for sharing with your friends, best served with cocktails and a girlie film.

PINK CHAMPAGNE CUPCAKES

I love having all my girlfriends round to my house. We get together often and have a good old gossip and do girlie things like painting our nails and having facials. These cupcakes are perfect for a bit of added glamour and indulgence on a girls' night in.

PREPARATION TIME: 25 MINUTES
BAKING TIME: 20 MINUTES
MAKES 12 CAKES

FOR THE CUPCAKES
230G UNSALTED BUTTER, SOFTENED
230G CASTER SUGAR
4 EGGS
230G SELF-RAISING FLOUR, SIFTED
2 TEASPOONS BAKING POWDER
230G STRAWBERRIES, HULLED AND FINELY
CHOPPED
4 TABLESPOONS PINK CHAMPAGNE

FOR THE BUTTERCREAM
255G ICING SUGAR, SIFTED
115G UNSALTED BUTTER, SOFTENED
1 TABLESPOON MILK
1-2 TABLESPOONS PINK CHAMPAGNE
A FEW DROPS OF PINK FOOD COLOURING

TO DECORATE
PINK SUGAR SAND, TO SPRINKLE
EDIBLE GLITTER

**EQUIPMENT: MIXER, 12-HOLE MUFFIN TIN
LINED WITH MUFFIN CASES, PIPING BAG
FITTED WITH LARGE STAR NOZZLE**

Preheat the oven to 160°C/325°F/Gas Mark 3.

Using a mixer, whisk together the butter and caster sugar until light and creamy. Add the eggs and whisk again. Fold in the flour and baking powder, using a spatula. Add the strawberry pieces and champagne to the batter and fold in very gently. Divide the cake mixture between the muffin cases and bake for 20 minutes, until the cakes are firm and spring back to your touch. Transfer to a rack to cool.

For the icing, whisk together the icing sugar, butter, milk, champagne and food colouring to make a pale pink frosting. Spoon into the piping bag and pipe a large swirl on to each cooled cake. Decorate with a sprinkle of pink sugar sand and a little edible glitter for extra sparkle.

The cakes will keep for up to 3 days if stored in an airtight container.

JELLY SHOT CUPCAKES

As you may know, I can be a party girl! There are few things I like better than a night out on the tiles, dancing with my girlfriends. These are the perfect pre-night-out snack to get the party started – cupcakes filled with a wicked tequila jelly.

Make the jelly up according to the packet instructions but replace half the water with tequila, and add the juice of 2 limes. Once the jelly is dissolved, leave to set in the refrigerator.

Preheat the oven to 160°C/325°F/Gas Mark 3.

Using a mixer, whisk together the butter and caster sugar until light and creamy. Add the eggs and whisk again. Gently fold in the flour, baking powder, vanilla, lime juice and zest, tequila and salt, using a spatula.

Divide the mixture between the muffin cases and bake for 20 minutes, until the cakes are firm and spring back to your touch. Transfer to a rack to cool.

When the cakes are cool, use a cupcake plunger or a sharp knife to remove the centre of each cupcake and fill them with a spoonful of jelly, discarding the removed cake. (You can use these discarded cake crumbs to make truffles or to sprinkle over ice cream if you wish.)

For the buttercream, whisk together the icing sugar, butter, milk, tequila and salt to make a smooth, stiff frosting. Colour it a pale minty green colour by whisking in a few drops of food colouring. Spoon it into the piping bag and pipe a swirl on top of each cake.

Peel thin strands of zest from some of the limes, then cut the limes into wedges and dip them in the rock salt. Place a lime wedge on top of each cake and decorate with the lime zest. Your guests should suck the salty lime and then eat the cupcake for a tequila slammer effect.

PREPARATION TIME: 25 MINUTES
BAKING TIME: 20 MINUTES
MAKES 12 CAKES

FOR THE TEQUILA LIME JELLY
1 PACKET OF LIME JELLY (135G)
APPROX. 300ML TEQUILA
JUICE OF 2 LIMES

FOR THE CUPCAKES
200G UNSALTED BUTTER, SOFTENED
220G CASTER SUGAR
4 EGGS
220G SELF-RAISING FLOUR, SIFTED
2 TEASPOONS BAKING POWDER
2 TEASPOONS VANILLA BEAN PASTE OR
   VANILLA EXTRACT
JUICE AND FINELY GRATED ZEST OF 6 LIMES
6 TABLESPOONS TEQUILA
2 TEASPOONS SEA SALT FLAKES

FOR THE BUTTERCREAM
300G ICING SUGAR, SIFTED
150G UNSALTED BUTTER, SOFTENED
1–2 TABLESPOONS WHOLE MILK
2 TABLESPOONS TEQUILA
SALT TO TASTE
A FEW DROPS OF GREEN FOOD COLOURING

TO DECORATE
4 LIMES, ROCK SALT

**EQUIPMENT: MIXER, 12-HOLE MUFFIN TIN
LINED WITH MUFFIN CASES, CUPCAKE
PLUNGER OR SHARP KNIFE, PIPING BAG
FITTED WITH LARGE STAR NOZZLE**

CHOCOLATE FONDUE CUPCAKES

These make a great dessert to serve on a girls' night in – what group of girls doesn't enjoy cake dunked in rich chocolate sauce? If you want to offer some healthy snacks as part of the meal, you can dip strawberries and grapes into the fondue alongside the mini cupcakes.

PREPARATION TIME: 25 MINUTES
BAKING TIME: 8-10 MINUTES
SERVES 8

FOR THE CUPCAKES
50G UNSALTED BUTTER, SOFTENED
50G CASTER SUGAR
50G LIGHT BROWN SUGAR
2 EGGS
80G SELF-RAISING FLOUR, SIFTED
30G COCOA POWDER, SIFTED
½ TEASPOON BICARBONATE OF SODA
40ML SOURED CREAM
1 TEASPOON VANILLA BEAN PASTE
A PINCH OF SALT

FOR THE FONDUE
400G DARK CHOCOLATE
85G UNSALTED BUTTER
250ML DOUBLE CREAM
50ML MILK
2 TABLESPOONS GOLDEN SYRUP

EQUIPMENT: MIXER, 24-HOLE MINI MUFFIN TIN LINED WITH MINI MUFFIN CASES, FONDUE POT AND SKEWERS

Preheat the oven to 160°C/325°F/Gas Mark 3.

Using a mixer, whisk together the butter, caster sugar and light brown sugar until light and creamy. Add the eggs and whisk again. Gently fold in the flour, cocoa powder, bicarbonate of soda, soured cream, vanilla bean paste and salt, using a spatula.

Divide the cake mixture between the mini muffin cases and bake for 8–10 minutes, until the cakes are firm and spring back to your touch. Transfer to a rack to cool.

For the fondue, place all the ingredients in a heatproof bowl over a pan of simmering water and leave until the chocolate has melted. Stir so that the ingredients all combine and the sauce is thick and glossy. Transfer to a fondue pot to serve, if you have one; if not, just serve straight from the bowl. The fondue will stay warm enough to serve in this way for about 15 minutes. Plenty of time to dunk your cakes and fruit and indulge!

PINA COLADA CUPCAKES

I love going away on girlie holidays – there are few things nicer than lying by the side of a tropical pool getting tanned in a bikini, reading some good chick-lit and sipping pina colada cocktails. Serve these cakes with cocktail umbrellas for true holiday effect.

PREPARATION TIME: 25 MINUTES
BAKING TIME: 20 MINUTES
MAKES 16 CAKES

FOR THE CAKES
200G UNSALTED BUTTER, SOFTENED
90G BROWN SUGAR
340G CASTER SUGAR
4 EGGS
560G SELF-RAISING FLOUR, SIFTED
2 TEASPOONS BAKING POWDER
1½ TEASPOONS BICARBONATE OF SODA
6 TABLESPOONS COCONUT MILK
4 TABLESPOONS MALIBU OR OTHER
   COCONUT LIQUEUR
1 X 400G TIN OF PINEAPPLE PIECES,
   DRAINED AND FINELY CHOPPED
100G DESICCATED COCONUT

**FOR THE COCONUT CREAM CHEESE
FROSTING**
450–500G ICING SUGAR, SIFTED
50G UNSALTED BUTTER, SOFTENED
180G CREAM CHEESE
2 TABLESPOONS MALIBU OR OTHER
   COCONUT LIQUEUR
2 TABLESPOONS COCONUT MILK
½ TEASPOON COCONUT ESSENCE

TO DECORATE
DRIED PINEAPPLE PIECES
PAPER COCKTAIL UMBRELLAS

**EQUIPMENT: MIXER, 12- AND 6-HOLE MUFFIN
TINS LINED WITH MUFFIN CASES, PIPING
BAG FITTED WITH LARGE STAR NOZZLE**

Preheat the oven to 160°C/325°F/Gas Mark 3.

Using a mixer, whisk together the butter, brown sugar and caster sugar until light and creamy. Add the eggs and whisk again. Gently fold in the flour, baking powder, bicarbonate of soda, coconut milk, Malibu, pineapple pieces and desiccated coconut, using a spatula.

Divide the mixture between the muffin cases and bake for 20 minutes, until the cakes are firm and spring back to your touch. Transfer to a rack to cool.

For the cream cheese frosting, whisk 450g of the icing sugar with the butter, cream cheese, Malibu, coconut milk and coconut essence. If the icing is too soft, gradually add the remaining icing sugar until you have a stiff icing. Spoon it into the piping bag and pipe a swirl on top of each cake.

Decorate each cake with some dried pineapple and an umbrella.

PIMM'S LAYER CAKE

This giant layer cake contains delicate layers of ginger ale and Pimm's-scented sponge filled with 4 different Pimm's-inspired buttercreams and topped with fresh fruit. It's one of the best summery cakes I know.

PREPARATION TIME: 25 MINUTES

BAKING TIME: 45 MINS – 1 HOUR

FOR THE CAKES

440G UNSALTED BUTTER, SOFTENED

440G CASTER SUGAR

6 EGGS

440G SELF-RAISING FLOUR, SIFTED

4 TEASPOONS BAKING POWDER

30G CRYSTALLIZED GINGER, FINELY
CHOPPED

3 TABLESPOONS GINGER ALE

4 TABLESPOONS PIMM'S

FOR THE BASIC BUTTERCREAM

1KG ICING SUGAR, SIFTED

500G UNSALTED BUTTER, SOFTENED

4–6 TABLESPOONS WHOLE MILK

FOR THE CUCUMBER BUTTERCREAM

20G FINELY CHOPPED CUCUMBER SKIN

PURÉE FROM 1 LARGE PEELED CUCUMBER

A FEW DROPS OF GREEN FOOD
COLOURING

A SPLASH OF PIMM'S

FOR THE STRAWBERRY BUTTERCREAM

1 TEASPOON STRAWBERRY ESSENCE

A FEW DROPS OF PINK FOOD
COLOURING

A SPLASH OF PIMM'S

FOR THE MINT BUTTERCREAM

1 TABLESPOON FINELY CHOPPED MINT
LEAVES

1 TEASPOON MINT ESSENCE

A FEW DROPS OF GREEN FOOD
COLOURING

A SPLASH OF PIMM'S

FOR THE ORANGE BUTTERCREAM

ZEST AND RIND OF 1 ORANGE

1 TEASPOON ORANGE ESSENCE

A FEW DROPS OF ORANGE FOOD
COLOURING

A SPLASH OF PIMM'S

TO DECORATE

FRESH STRAWBERRIES AND ORANGE
SLICES

CUCUMBER SLICES

MINT LEAVES

**EQUIPMENT: MIXER, 2 X 20CM ROUND
SANDWICH CAKE TINS, GREASED AND
LINED**

Preheat the oven to 160°C/325°F/Gas Mark 3.

Using a mixer, whisk together the butter and caster sugar until light and creamy. Add the eggs and whisk again. Gently fold in the flour, baking powder, chopped ginger and ginger ale, using a spatula.

Spoon the cake mixture into the two cake tins and bake for 45 minutes – 1 hour, until the cakes are firm to touch and a skewer inserted into the centre comes out clean, with no cake batter on it. When you have removed the cakes from the oven, make small holes over the top of each one using a skewer and drizzle over the Pimm's so that it soaks into the holes. Leave to cool in the tins.

For the icing, whisk together the icing sugar, butter and enough milk to make a smooth, stiff frosting. Divide the mixture between 4 bowls, one for each of the flavoured icings.

Add the finely chopped cucumber skin and the cucumber purée to the first bowl, with a few drops of green food colouring. Add a splash of Pimm's and mix well.

Add the strawberry essence and a few drops of pink food colouring to the second bowl. Add a splash of Pimm's and mix well.

Add the mint, mint essence and a few drops of green food colouring to the third bowl. Add a splash of Pimm's and mix well.

Finally, add the orange zest and rind, orange essence and a few drops of orange food colouring to the fourth bowl. Add a splash of Pimm's and mix well.

After the cakes have cooled and are soaked in Pimm's, cut each one in half to make 4 cake layers. Using a knife, spread a thick layer of buttercream between the layers so that each layer has a different flavour: cucumber, strawberry, mint. Spread the orange icing over the top and round the sides of the cake and decorate with strawberries, cucumber, mint leaves and orange slices. Serve straight away, with a glass of Pimm's on the side.

STRAWBERRY DAIQUIRI CUPCAKES

When strawberries are ripe and juicy in the summer, I adore making these cupcakes for lazy afternoon barbecues in the garden. They are great to serve with strawberry daiquiri cocktails.

PREPARATION TIME: 25 MINUTES
BAKING TIME: 20 MINUTES
MAKES 12 CAKES

FOR THE CUPCAKES
200G UNSALTED BUTTER, SOFTENED
220G CASTER SUGAR
4 EGGS
220G SELF-RAISING FLOUR, SIFTED
2 TEASPOONS BAKING POWDER
4 TEASPOONS STRAWBERRY ESSENCE
  (YOU'LL FIND THIS IN THE BAKING
  SECTION OF YOUR SUPERMARKET)
ZEST OF 2 LIMES
500G STRAWBERRIES, HULLED AND
  CHOPPED

FOR THE CRÈME CHANTILLY
500ML DOUBLE CREAM
100G ICING SUGAR, SIFTED

TO DECORATE
STRAWBERRY SCHNAPPS
12 STRAWBERRIES

**EQUIPMENT: MIXER, 12-HOLE MUFFIN TIN
LINED WITH MUFFIN CASES, PIPING BAG
FITTED WITH LARGE STAR NOZZLE**

Preheat the oven to 160°C/325°F/Gas Mark 3.

Using a mixer, whisk together the butter and caster sugar until light and creamy. Add the eggs and whisk again. Gently fold in the flour, baking powder, strawberry essence, lime zest and strawberry pieces, using a spatula.

Divide the mixture between the muffin cases and bake for 20 minutes, until the cakes are firm and spring back to your touch. Transfer to a rack to cool.

For the crème Chantilly, place the cream and icing sugar in a mixing bowl and whisk to stiff peaks.

When you are ready to serve, drizzle each cupcake with a little strawberry schnapps. Spoon the crème Chantilly into the piping bag and pipe swirls on top of each cake. Decorate each cake with a whole strawberry. As these cakes contain fresh cream, they are best eaten on the day they are made and should be stored in the refrigerator if you are not serving them straight away.

NAUGHTY CUPCAKES

The cakes in this chapter are cheeky, romantic or just a little bit wild!

LIPSTICK AND LIPS CUPCAKES

I love these bright pink cakes topped with sugarcraft lipsticks and lips, all coated in my signature glitter. Cupcakes don't get much more glamorous than this.

PREPARATION TIME: 25 MINUTES

BAKING TIME: 20 MINUTES

MAKES 12 CAKES

FOR THE CUPCAKES

200G UNSALTED BUTTER, SOFTENED

220G CASTER SUGAR

4 EGGS

220G SELF-RAISING FLOUR, SIFTED

2 TEASPOONS BAKING POWDER

2 TEASPOONS VANILLA BEAN PASTE OR

VANILLA EXTRACT

FOR THE BUTTERCREAM

300G ICING SUGAR, SIFTED

150G UNSALTED BUTTER, SOFTENED

A FEW DROPS OF PINK FOOD COLOURING

1–2 TABLESPOONS WHOLE MILK

TO DECORATE

ICING SUGAR, FOR DUSTING

150G WHITE READY-TO-ROLL ICING

FOOD COLOURING

LUSTRE POWDER

EDIBLE GLITTER

EQUIPMENT: MIXER, 12-HOLE MUFFIN TIN LINED WITH MUFFIN CASES, LIPS AND LIPSTICK SILICONE MOULDS, SILICONE MAT OR BAKING PARCHMENT, PIPING BAG FITTED WITH LARGE STAR NOZZLE

Begin by preparing the lips and lipstick decorations, as they need to dry before being used. Coat the silicone moulds with a small amount of vegetable oil to prevent sticking. Take small pieces of the ready-to-roll icing and press them into the moulds so that they take the shape of lipsticks and lips. Remove from the moulds and place on a silicone mat or a sheet of baking parchment to dry, trimming any excess icing with a sharp knife. Repeat with all the remaining icing. Leave the icing to set for 24 hours. Once the icing is dry, paint the decorations with food colouring or lustre powder.

Preheat the oven to 160°C/325°F/Gas Mark 3.

Using a mixer, whisk together the butter and caster sugar until light and creamy. Add the eggs and whisk again. Gently fold in the flour, baking powder and vanilla bean paste, using a spatula.

Divide the mixture between the muffin cases. Bake for 20 minutes, until the cakes are firm and spring back to your touch. Transfer to a rack to cool.

For the icing, whisk together the icing sugar, butter, a few drops of food colouring and enough milk to make a smooth, stiff frosting. Spoon into the piping bag and pipe a swirl on to each cake. Decorate with lips or a lipstick and sprinkle with edible glitter.

The cakes will keep for up to 3 days if stored in an airtight container.

SUGAR HEART VALENTINE CUPCAKES

On Valentine's Day why not make these cakes for the one you secretly love - or, failing that, for your friends and family to show them how much you care. Topped with a wicked marshmallow topping and sugar hearts, these are the prettiest of cupcakes.

PREPARATION TIME: 30 MINUTES

BAKING TIME: 20 MINUTES

MAKES 12 CAKES

FOR THE CUPCAKES

100G UNSALTED BUTTER, SOFTENED

100G CASTER SUGAR

100G LIGHT BROWN SUGAR

4 EGGS

160G SELF-RAISING FLOUR, SIFTED

60G COCOA POWDER, SIFTED

1 TEASPOON BICARBONATE OF SODA

4 TEASPOONS RASPBERRY ESSENCE

80ML SOURED CREAM

A PINCH OF SALT

FOR THE MARSHMALLOW TOPPING

250G CASTER SUGAR

3 EGG WHITES

2 TABLESPOONS COLD WATER

TO DECORATE

SUGAR LOVE HEARTS

EQUIPMENT: MIXER, 12-HOLE MUFFIN TIN LINED WITH MUFFIN CASES, SUGAR THERMOMETER, PIPING BAG FITTED WITH LARGE STAR NOZZLE

Preheat the oven to 160°C/325°F/Gas Mark 3.

Using a mixer, whisk together the butter, caster sugar and light brown sugar until light and creamy. Add the eggs and whisk again. Gently fold in the flour, cocoa powder, bicarbonate of soda, raspberry essence, soured cream and salt, using a spatula.

Divide the mixture between the muffin cases. Bake for 20 minutes, until the cakes are firm and spring back to your touch. Transfer to a rack to cool.

For the marshmallow topping, place the caster sugar, egg whites and water in a saucepan and heat to 60°C, whisking continuously. Once the mixture reaches 60°C, transfer it to a mixer with whisk attachment and whisk until white and glossy peaks are formed. Pipe swirls on top of each cake.

Heat the grill and place the cupcakes under it for a few seconds to toast the topping. Alternatively you can do this with a chef's blowtorch. Take care that the meringue does not burn. Decorate each cake with a sugar love heart and serve straight away.

TORSO AND CORSET CUPCAKES

These cakes have real sex appeal. Torso and corset silicone moulds are available in cookware shops and online.

PREPARATION TIME: 25 MINUTES
BAKING TIME: 20 MINUTES
MAKES 12 CAKES

FOR THE CUPCAKES
200G UNSALTED BUTTER, SOFTENED
220G CASTER SUGAR
4 EGGS
220G SELF-RAISING FLOUR, SIFTED
2 TEASPOONS BAKING POWDER
2 TEASPOONS VANILLA BEAN PASTE OR
VANILLA EXTRACT

FOR THE BUTTERCREAM
300G ICING SUGAR, SIFTED
150G UNSALTED BUTTER, SOFTENED
1–2 TABLESPOONS WHOLE MILK

TO DECORATE
ICING SUGAR, FOR DUSTING
150G WHITE READY-TO-ROLL ICING
FOOD COLOURING
LUSTRE POWDER
SUGAR PEARLS
EDIBLE GLITTER

**EQUIPMENT: MIXER, 12-HOLE MUFFIN TIN
LINED WITH MUFFIN CASES, TORSO AND
CORSET SILICONE MOULDS, SILICONE
MAT OR BAKING PARCHMENT, PIPING BAG
FITTED WITH LARGE ROUND NOZZLE**

Begin by preparing the decorations, as they need to dry before being used. Dust the silicone moulds with a little icing sugar so that the decorations do not stick. Take small pieces of the ready-to-roll icing and press them into the moulds so that they take the shape of torsos and corsets. Remove from the moulds and place on a silicone mat or sheet of baking parchment to dry, trimming any excess icing with a sharp knife. Repeat with all the remaining icing. Leave the icing to set for 24 hours. Once the icing is dry, paint the decorations with food colouring or lustre powder and fix on sugar pearls for extra decoration if you wish.

Preheat the oven to 160°C/325°F/Gas Mark 3.

Using a mixer, whisk together the butter and caster sugar until light and creamy. Add the eggs and whisk again. Gently fold in the flour, baking powder and vanilla bean paste, using a spatula.

Divide the mixture between the muffin cases. Bake for 20 minutes, until the cakes are firm and spring back to your touch. Transfer to a rack to cool.

For the buttercream, whisk together the icing sugar, butter and enough milk to make a smooth, stiff frosting. Spoon it into the piping bag and pipe a swirl on to each cupcake. Decorate the cakes with a torso or corset and sprinkle with edible glitter.

The cakes will keep for up to 3 days if stored in an airtight container.

HEN PARTY CUPCAKES

To celebrate one of your best girlfriends getting married, why not make a batch of these kinky cupcakes for her hen party? You can be as wild as you dare with the decorations!

PREPARATION TIME: 30 MINUTES

BAKING TIME: 20 MINUTES

MAKES 12 CAKES

FOR THE CUPCAKES

100G UNSALTED BUTTER, SOFTENED

100G CASTER SUGAR

100G LIGHT BROWN SUGAR

4 EGGS

160G SELF-RAISING FLOUR, SIFTED

60G COCOA POWDER, SIFTED

1 TEASPOON BICARBONATE OF SODA

80ML SOURED CREAM

2 TEASPOONS VANILLA BEAN PASTE

A PINCH OF SALT

FOR THE BUTTERCREAM

300G ICING SUGAR, SIFTED

40G COCOA POWDER, SIFTED

150G UNSALTED BUTTER, SOFTENED

60ML MILK

TO DECORATE

200G WHITE READY-TO-ROLL ICING

RED, PINK, BLACK FOOD COLOURINGS

BLACK SUGAR PEARL BEADS

EDIBLE GLITTER (OPTIONAL)

EDIBLE GLUE

EQUIPMENT: MIXER, 12-HOLE MUFFIN TIN LINED WITH MUFFIN CASES, PIPING BAG FITTED WITH LARGE STAR NOZZLE, SMALL SQUARE CUTTER, LETTER L CUTTER, SMALL ROUND CUTTER, SMALL HEART CUTTER

Preheat the oven to 160°C/325°F/Gas Mark 3.

Using a mixer, whisk together the butter, caster sugar and light brown sugar until light and creamy. Add the eggs and whisk again. Gently fold in the flour, cocoa powder, bicarbonate of soda, soured cream, vanilla bean paste and salt, using a spatula.

Divide the mixture between the muffin cases and bake for 20 minutes, until the cakes are firm and spring back to your touch. Transfer to a rack to cool.

For the icing, whisk together the icing sugar, cocoa powder, butter and milk to make a rich chocolate frosting. Spread a thick layer over the top of each cake, using a palette knife.

For the decorations, roll out some of the white ready-to-roll icing and use a square cutter to cut out squares measuring about 5cm. Set aside. Colour some more of the ready-to-roll icing red, then roll it out thinly and cut out L-shapes, using the cutter. Fix the red Ls on top of the white squares, using a little edible glue. You can do these with pink Ls in place of the red ones if you prefer. Place the L plates on top of the cakes.

To make handcuffs, colour some more of the ready-to-roll icing black. Roll the icing into little sausages and join the ends to make rings. Cut out a square of rolled-out white or red icing. Place 2 rings on top of each square, then, using black sugar pearl beads, create a chain in the middle to connect them, fixing them in place with edible glue if needed. Place a square on top of each cake. (continued overleaf)

To make hearts, colour some more of the ready-to-roll icing pink or red and roll out thinly on a surface dusted with icing sugar. Using the heart cutter, cut out heart shapes. Following the steps above, make some more round icing discs and fix hearts in pretty patterns on top of them, using edible glue. Place a heart disc on top of each cake.

The cakes will keep for up to 3 days if stored in an airtight container.

PICNIC IN THE PARK CAKES

This chapter contains fun and transportable cakes that are perfect for an afternoon picnic on a summer's day. With a rug, a bottle of fizz and some delicious homemade cakes, what better way to spend an afternoon?

ICE CREAM CONE CAKES

My daughter Dixie just adores these cakes. We always take them for picnics in the park – they are an easy way to impress other mums and a massive crowd always gathers when I serve them. Dixie loves hers drizzled with strawberry sauce, and my preference is always chocolate.

Preheat the oven to 150°C/300°F/Gas Mark 2.

Whisk the butter and sugar together in a bowl until light and creamy. Beat in the eggs until fully incorporated. Sift the flour and baking powder into the bowl and fold into the butter mixture with the vanilla bean paste, using a spatula, until fully incorporated. Spoon the mixture into the piping bag with the large round nozzle.

Wrap a small piece of foil around the base of each cornet to ensure it doesn't burn and place them on the baking tray.

Pipe the cake mixture into each cornet until approximately three-quarters full, leaving about 2–3 cm below the rim of the cornet to allow room for the cake to rise. Carefully transport the tray to the oven and bake for 30–35 minutes, until the cakes are firm and spring back to your touch. Remove from the oven and leave to cool on the tray.

To prepare the buttercream, whisk the icing sugar with the butter and milk in a large bowl for about 3–5 minutes, until light and creamy, adding a little more milk if the mixture is too stiff. Spoon the icing into the piping bag fitted with the large star nozzle and pipe a large swirl of icing on to each cornet. Pipe the icing so it looks like a Mr Whippy ice cream – don't be shy of piling the icing really high for best effect. Decorate with rainbow-coloured sugar strands and push a chocolate flake into the icing on each cake. Just before serving, drizzle over a little strawberry or chocolate sauce, if you like.

The cakes will keep for up to 3 days if stored in an airtight container.

PREPARATION TIME: 25 MINUTES
BAKING TIME: 30–35 MINUTES
MAKES 12 CAKES

FOR THE ICE CREAM CONE CAKES
230G UNSALTED BUTTER, SOFTENED
230G CASTER SUGAR
4 EGGS
230G SELF-RAISING FLOUR
2 TEASPOONS BAKING POWDER
2 TEASPOONS VANILLA BEAN PASTE
12 ICE CREAM CUP CORNETS (SUCH AS ASKEYS)

FOR THE BUTTERCREAM
400G ICING SUGAR, SIFTED
200G UNSALTED BUTTER, SOFTENED
1 TABLESPOON MILK

TO DECORATE
RAINBOW SUGAR STRANDS
12 CHOCOLATE FLAKES
CHOCOLATE OR STRAWBERRY SAUCE (OPTIONAL)

EQUIPMENT: BAKING TRAY, SILVER FOIL, PIPING BAG WITH LARGE STAR NOZZLE

MILKSHAKE CUPCAKES

These cakes are inspired by the popular Mini Milk ice lollies, and are topped with pastel icing and jelly milk bottles. These are great to serve as mini cupcakes, if you prefer, ideal for large parties or as sweet canapés.

PREPARATION TIME: 40 MINUTES

BAKING TIME: 20 MINUTES PER
   BATCH OF CAKES

MAKES 36 CAKES

FOR THE STRAWBERRY CUPCAKES

100G UNSALTED BUTTER, SOFTENED

220G CASTER SUGAR

4 EGGS

220G SELF-RAISING FLOUR, SIFTED

2 TEASPOONS BAKING POWDER

400G STRAWBERRIES, HULLED AND
   CHOPPED

2 TEASPOONS STRAWBERRY ESSENCE

A FEW DROPS OF PINK FOOD COLOURING

10 TABLESPOONS DOUBLE CREAM

FOR THE STRAWBERRY BUTTERCREAM

300G ICING SUGAR, SIFTED

150G UNSALTED BUTTER, SOFTENED

1–2 TABLESPOONS DOUBLE CREAM

1 TEASPOON VANILLA BEAN PASTE

A FEW DROPS OF PINK FOOD COLOURING

For the strawberry mini milk cakes

Preheat the oven to 160°C/325°F/Gas Mark 3.

Using a mixer, whisk together the butter and caster sugar until light and creamy. Add the eggs and whisk again. Gently fold in the flour, baking powder, chopped strawberries, strawberry essence, pink food colouring and double cream, using a spatula.

Spoon the cake mixture into one tray of muffin cases and bake for 20 minutes, until the cakes are firm and spring back to your touch. Transfer to a rack to cool.

For the buttercream, whisk together the icing sugar, butter, vanilla bean paste and double cream to make a smooth, stiff icing. Colour it pink with a few drops of food colouring. Spoon the icing into one of the piping bags and pipe a swirl on to each cake. Decorate with mini milk bottle sweets.

FOR THE CHOCOLATE CUPCAKES

100G UNSALTED BUTTER, SOFTENED
100G CASTER SUGAR
100G LIGHT BROWN SUGAR
4 EGGS
160G SELF-RAISING FLOUR, SIFTED
60G COCOA POWDER, SIFTED
1 TEASPOON BICARBONATE OF SODA
80ML DOUBLE CREAM
2 TEASPOONS VANILLA BEAN PASTE
A PINCH OF SALT

FOR THE CHOCOLATE BUTTERCREAM

300G ICING SUGAR, SIFTED
150G UNSALTED BUTTER, SOFTENED
1–2 TABLESPOONS DOUBLE CREAM
30G COCOA POWDER, SIFTED

FOR THE VANILLA CUPCAKES

100G UNSALTED BUTTER, SOFTENED
220G CASTER SUGAR
4 EGGS
220G SELF-RAISING FLOUR, SIFTED
2 TEASPOONS BAKING POWDER
SEEDS FROM 1 VANILLA POD
10 TABLESPOONS DOUBLE CREAM

FOR THE VANILLA BUTTERCREAM

300G ICING SUGAR, SIFTED
150G UNSALTED BUTTER, SOFTENED
1–2 TABLESPOONS DOUBLE CREAM
1 TEASPOON VANILLA BEAN PASTE
A FEW DROPS OF BLUE FOOD COLOURING

TO DECORATE

MINI MILK BOTTLE SWEETS

EQUIPMENT: MIXER, 3 X 12-HOLE MUFFIN
TINS LINED WITH MUFFIN CASES, 3 PIPING
BAGS FITTED WITH LARGE STAR NOZZLES

For the chocolate mini milk cakes

Preheat the oven to 160°C/325°F/Gas Mark 3.

Using a mixer, whisk together the butter, caster sugar and light brown sugar until light and creamy. Add the eggs and whisk again. Gently fold in the flour, cocoa powder and bicarbonate of soda, double cream, vanilla bean paste and salt, using a spatula.

Spoon the cake mixture into the second tray of muffin cases and bake for 20 minutes, until the cakes are firm and spring back to your touch. Transfer to a rack to cool.

For the buttercream, whisk together the icing sugar, butter, double cream and cocoa powder to make a smooth, stiff icing. Spoon the icing into one of the piping bags and pipe a swirl on to each cake. Decorate with mini milk bottle sweets.

For the vanilla mini milk cakes

Preheat the oven to 160°C/325°F/Gas Mark 3.

Using a mixer, whisk together the butter and caster sugar until light and creamy. Add the eggs and whisk again. Gently fold in the flour, baking powder, seeds from the vanilla pod and double cream, using a spatula.

Spoon the cake mixture into the final tray of muffin cases and bake for 20 minutes, until the cakes are firm and spring back to your touch. Transfer to a rack to cool.

For the buttercream, whisk together the icing sugar, butter, vanilla bean paste and double cream to make a smooth, stiff frosting. Colour it blue with a few drops of food colouring. Spoon it into one of the piping bags and pipe a swirl on to each cake. Decorate with mini milk bottle sweets.

The cakes will keep for up to 3 days if stored in an airtight container.

ALICE IN WONDERLAND 'EAT ME' CUPCAKES

Alice in Wonderland is one of Dixie's favourite stories, and I like to make these cakes for her so that we can eat them and pretend to fall down the rabbit-hole together.

PREPARATION TIME: 25 MINUTES
BAKING TIME: 20 MINUTES
MAKES 12 CAKES

FOR THE CUPCAKES
200G UNSALTED BUTTER, SOFTENED
220G CASTER SUGAR
4 EGGS
220G SELF-RAISING FLOUR, SIFTED
2 TEASPOONS BAKING POWDER
2 TEASPOONS VANILLA BEAN PASTE OR
   VANILLA EXTRACT
ZEST AND JUICE OF 6 LEMONS
FEW DROPS OF YELLOW FOOD COLOURING

FOR THE DRIZZLE
100G WHITE CASTER SUGAR
JUICE OF 4 LEMONS

FOR THE BUTTERCREAM
300G ICING SUGAR, SIFTED
150G UNSALTED BUTTER, SOFTENED
JUICE OF 2 LEMONS
1–2 TABLESPOONS WHOLE MILK
FEW DROPS OF YELLOW FOOD COLOURING

TO DECORATE
250G READY-TO-ROLL FONDANT ICING
FOOD COLOURING OF YOUR CHOOSING
ICING SUGAR FOR DUSTING
200G ROYAL ICING SUGAR
EDIBLE GLITTER

**EQUIPMENT: MIXER, 12-HOLE MUFFIN TIN
LINED WITH MUFFIN CASES, RECTANGULAR
CUTTER, SHARP KNIFE, PIPING BAG FITTED
WITH SMALL ROUND NOZZLE**

Begin by preparing the decorations, as they need to dry before being used. Colour the fondant icing with food colouring of your choosing. On a surface dusted with icing sugar, roll out the fondant and cut out 12 rectangles of icing. Using the sharp knife, cut off 2 edges to make a luggage-tag shape. Place them on a sheet of greaseproof paper or a silicone mat. Make up the royal icing according to the packet instructions – it should be stiff and hold a peak when you lift the beaters. Spoon it into the piping bag and carefully write 'Eat Me' on each of the rectangles, then sprinkle with edible glitter. Leave to dry overnight.

Preheat the oven to 160°C/325°F/Gas Mark 3.

Using a mixer, whisk together the butter and caster sugar until light and creamy. Add the eggs and whisk again. Gently fold in the flour, baking powder, vanilla bean paste and the lemon juice and zest, using a spatula. Colour the batter pale yellow with a few drops of yellow food colouring.

Divide the mixture between the muffin cases and bake for 20 minutes, until the cakes are firm and spring back to your touch.

Put the caster sugar and lemon juice for the drizzle into a small saucepan and heat until the sugar has dissolved. Take off the heat, then poke holes in the top of each cupcake with a small skewer and pour over the lemon drizzle. Transfer to a rack to cool.

For the icing, whisk together the icing sugar, butter, lemon juice and enough milk to make a smooth, stiff frosting. Whisk in a few drops of food colouring to colour it pale yellow. Spread the icing over the top of each cake and decorate each one with a sugar 'Eat Me' label.

The cakes will keep for up to 3 days if stored in an airtight container.

BAKEWELL TART CUPCAKES

These cakes bring back memories of family picnics and eating Mr Kipling cherry Bakewell tarts when I was young. I have to say that these cupcakes are a bit more refined, with a delicate almond sponge packed with cherries and topped with a grown-up amaretto icing and a glacé cherry. They are the perfect picnic treat.

PREPARATION TIME: 25 MINUTES

BAKING TIME: 20 MINUTES

MAKES 12 CAKES

FOR THE CUPCAKES

200G UNSALTED BUTTER, SOFTENED

220G CASTER SUGAR

4 EGGS

220G SELF-RAISING FLOUR, SIFTED

100G GROUND ALMONDS

2 TEASPOONS BAKING POWDER

4 TEASPOONS ALMOND ESSENCE

200G GLACÉ CHERRIES, CHOPPED

8 TABLESPOONS RASPBERRY JAM

FOR THE BUTTERCREAM

300G ICING SUGAR, SIFTED

150G UNSALTED BUTTER, SOFTENED

2 TEASPOONS ALMOND EXTRACT

1 TABLESPOON AMARETTO LIQUEUR

1–2 TABLESPOONS WHOLE MILK

TO DECORATE

12 WHOLE GLACÉ CHERRIES

TOASTED FLAKED ALMONDS

EQUIPMENT: MIXER, 12-HOLE MUFFIN TIN LINED WITH MUFFIN CASES, CUPCAKE PLUNGER OR SHARP KNIFE, PIPING BAG FITTED WITH LARGE STAR NOZZLE

Preheat the oven to 160°C/325°F/Gas Mark 3.

Using a mixer, whisk together the butter and caster sugar until light and creamy. Add the eggs and whisk again. Gently fold in the flour, baking powder, almond essence, ground almonds and chopped cherries, using a spatula.

Divide the mixture between the muffin cases and bake for 20 minutes, until the cakes are firm and spring back to your touch. Transfer to a rack to cool.

When the cakes are cool, cut out a hole in the centre of each one using the cupcake plunger or a sharp knife, and place a spoonful of jam in each hole. Replace the removed cake and press down so that the jam is sealed inside the cake.

For the buttercream, whisk together the icing sugar, butter, almond extract, liqueur and enough milk to make a smooth, stiff frosting. Spoon it into the piping bag and pipe a swirl on top of each cake. Decorate each cake with a whole cherry and sprinkle with toasted almonds.

The cakes will keep for up to 3 days if stored in an airtight container.

VINTAGE CUPCAKES

I love vintage; old movies, over-the-top feathered hats, and the cupcakes in this chapter take inspiration from these things. These cupcakes are OTT and completely kitsch, inspired by Hollywood vintage glamour and days at the races, and I make no apologies for them – these are some of my favourite cakes.

PEARLS AND BROOCHES CUPCAKES

The vintage look is coming back into fashion, and these cupcakes are beautiful and delicate. They are a hit with everyone I serve them to. Using silicone moulds to make the decorations means they take no time at all, and the results are very impressive. They are a really easy way to create a great impact. These cakes are perfect for vintage weddings or shabby chic events. The shimmery lustre finish of the brooches gives them a true touch of class and sophistication.

PREPARATION TIME: 25 MINUTES

BAKING TIME: 20 MINUTES

MAKES 12 CAKES

FOR THE CUPCAKES

230G UNSALTED BUTTER, SOFTENED

230G CASTER SUGAR

4 EGGS

230G SELF-RAISING FLOUR, SIFTED

2 TEASPOONS BAKING POWDER

2 TABLESPOONS ROSE WATER

FOR THE ICING

250G FONDANT ICING SUGAR, SIFTED,
    PLUS EXTRA FOR DUSTING

1–2 TABLESPOONS ROSE WATER

TO DECORATE

150G WHITE READY-TO-ROLL ICING

BRONZE EDIBLE LUSTRE SPRAY

LARGE SUGAR PEARLS

SUGAR ROSES OR CRYSTALLIZED
    ROSE PETALS

**EQUIPMENT: MIXER, 12-HOLE MUFFIN
TIN LINED WITH MUFFIN CASES, PIPING
BAG FITTED WITH LARGE STAR NOZZLE,
BROOCH AND FRAME SILICONE MOULDS
(BOTH WIDELY AVAILABLE ONLINE)**

Begin by preparing the vintage decorations, as they need to dry before being used. Coat the silicone moulds with a little oil so that the decorations do not stick. Take small pieces of the ready-to-roll icing and press them into the moulds so that they take the shape of brooches and flowers. Remove from the moulds and place on a silicone mat or sheet of baking parchment to dry, trimming any excess icing with a sharp knife. Repeat with all the remaining icing. Leave the icing to set for 24 hours. Once the icing is dry, spray with bronze lustre to decorate.

Preheat the oven to 160°C/325°F/Gas Mark 3.

Using a mixer, whisk together the butter and caster sugar until light and creamy. Add the eggs and whisk again. Fold in the flour, baking powder and rose water using a spatula. Divide the cake mixture between the muffin cases and bake for 20 minutes, until the cakes are firm and spring back to your touch. Transfer to a rack to cool.

For the icing, mix together the icing sugar and rose water until you have a smooth, thick frosting. Pipe it over the top of the cakes and decorate with your choice of lustre brooches, sugar flowers, sugar pearls, sugar roses or crystallized rose petals. Leave the icing to set before serving.

The cakes will keep for up to 3 days if stored in an airtight container.

HIGH HATS

These 'high hat' cupcakes, decorated in Eliza Doolittle style with feathers and bows, make a spectacular centrepiece for any party.

PREPARATION TIME: 25 MINUTES

BAKING TIME: 20 MINUTES

MAKES 12 CAKES

FOR THE CUPCAKES

100G UNSALTED BUTTER, SOFTENED

100G CASTER SUGAR

100G LIGHT BROWN SUGAR

4 EGGS

160G SELF-RAISING FLOUR, SIFTED

60G COCOA POWDER, SIFTED

1 TEASPOON BICARBONATE OF SODA

80ML SOURED CREAM

2 TEASPOONS VANILLA BEAN PASTE

A PINCH OF SALT

FOR THE MARSHMALLOW TOPPING

250G CASTER SUGAR

3 EGG WHITES

2 TABLESPOONS COLD WATER

TO DECORATE

700G PLAIN CHOCOLATE

FEATHERS

EQUIPMENT: MIXER, 12-HOLE MUFFIN TIN LINED WITH MUFFIN CASES, SUGAR THERMOMETER, PIPING BAG FITTED WITH LARGE ROUND NOZZLE

Preheat the oven to 160°C/325°F/Gas Mark 3.

Using a mixer, whisk together the butter, caster sugar and light brown sugar until light and creamy. Add the eggs and whisk again. Gently fold in the flour, cocoa powder, vanilla bean paste, bicarbonate of soda, soured cream and salt using a spatula.

Divide the mixture between the muffin cases and bake for 20 minutes, until the cakes are firm and spring back to your touch. Transfer to a rack to cool.

For the marshmallow topping, place the caster sugar, egg whites and water in a saucepan and heat to 60°C, whisking continuously. Once it reaches 60°C, transfer it to a mixer with a whisk attachment and whisk until white and glossy peaks are formed.

Spoon the meringue into the piping bag and pipe four rings on to each cake, getting smaller and higher each time (see overleaf). Leave to set.

Place the chocolate in a heatproof bowl over a pan of simmering water and leave until the chocolate has melted. Once melted, pour the chocolate into a deep bowl. One by one, turn the cupcakes upside down and carefully dip them into the bowl so that the marshmallow is covered with chocolate (see page 85). You will not need all of the chocolate, but it needs to be this much so that you can dip the cakes properly. You can use any leftover chocolate to flavour other cake mixtures or icings if you wish. Before the chocolate sets, insert a brightly coloured feather into the top and put the cakes into the fridge for 10 minutes to cool. Repeat with all the remaining cakes.

The cakes will keep for up to 3 days if stored in an airtight container.

LAVENDER BUTTON CUPCAKES

Gone are the days of lavender being associated with old ladies – it's a great ingredient to add to cupcake batter, for a delicate floral flavour. Paired here with honey-flavoured buttercream and decorated with pretty pastel buttons, I love to serve these cupcakes to friends for afternoon tea.

Begin by preparing the buttons, as they need to dry before being used. Dust the silicone moulds with a little icing sugar so that the decorations do not stick. Take small pieces of the ready-to-roll icing and press them into the moulds so that they take the shape of buttons. Leave the icing in the mould for about 20 seconds, then carefully remove and place on a silicone mat or a sheet of baking parchment to dry. Repeat with all the remaining icing, making a variety of different-sized buttons. Colour the buttons with lustre spray or powder and leave to set overnight. Alternatively you can colour the fondant by kneading several drops of food colouring into the ready-to-roll icing before shaping in the moulds if you prefer. You can store the dried buttons for up to 3 weeks in a tin.

Preheat the oven to 160°C/325°F/Gas Mark 3.

Heat the milk and dried lavender in a saucepan until warm but not boiling. Remove from the heat and leave to cool. Once cooled, strain the milk and discard the lavender.

Using a mixer, whisk together the butter and caster sugar until light and creamy. Add the eggs and whisk again. Gently fold in the flour, baking powder, vanilla bean paste and lavender-infused milk, using a spatula.

Divide the mixture between the muffin cases and bake for 20 minutes, until the cakes are firm and spring back to your touch. Transfer to a rack to cool.

PREPARATION TIME: 25 MINUTES

BAKING TIME: 20 MINUTES

MAKES 12 CAKES

FOR THE CUPCAKES

200ML MILK

8 TABLESPOONS DRIED CULINARY
   LAVENDER

200G UNSALTED BUTTER, SOFTENED

220G CASTER SUGAR

4 EGGS

220G SELF-RAISING FLOUR, SIFTED

2 TEASPOONS BAKING POWDER

2 TEASPOONS VANILLA BEAN PASTE OR
   VANILLA EXTRACT

FOR THE BUTTERCREAM

300G ICING SUGAR, SIFTED

150G UNSALTED BUTTER, SOFTENED

2 TABLESPOONS RUNNY HONEY

1–2 TABLESPOONS WHOLE MILK

FEW DROPS OF PASTEL FOOD COLOURING
   OF YOUR CHOICE

TO DECORATE

250G WHITE READY-TO-ROLL ICING

ICING SUGAR, FOR DUSTING

PASTEL EDIBLE LUSTRE SPRAY OR EDIBLE
   LUSTRE POWDER OR FOOD COLOURING

EDIBLE GLITTER

**EQUIPMENT: MIXER, 12-HOLE MUFFIN TIN
LINED WITH MUFFIN CASES, SILICONE
BUTTON MOULD**

For the buttercream, whisk together the icing sugar, butter, honey and enough milk to make a smooth, stiff frosting. Colour it pale purple with a few drops of food colouring. Spoon it into the piping bag and pipe swirls on top of each cake. Decorate with the pretty pastel buttons.

The cakes will keep for up to 3 days if stored in an airtight container.

BAKING WITH DIXIE

Spending an afternoon with my four-year-old daughter, Dixie, in the kitchen is one of my favourite weekend pastimes. These are Dixie's best recipes and we have spent many happy hours together making them.

STRAWBERRY CUPCAKES

These are the pinkest of cakes - perfect for little girls - decorated with strawberry icing and swirls of strawberry laces. Little girls love these cakes! Put a mini strawberry on top for added wow factor! I love making them with Dixie, who piles the icing high and decorates them with as many sweets as she can possibly fit on.

PREPARATION TIME: 25 MINUTES

BAKING TIME: 20 MINUTES

MAKES 12 CAKES

FOR THE CUPCAKES
200G UNSALTED BUTTER, SOFTENED
220G CASTER SUGAR
4 EGGS
220G SELF-RAISING FLOUR, SIFTED
2 TEASPOONS BAKING POWDER
4 TEASPOONS VANILLA BEAN PASTE OR
   VANILLA EXTRACT
A FEW DROPS OF PINK FOOD COLOURING

FOR THE BUTTERCREAM
300G ICING SUGAR, SIFTED
150G UNSALTED BUTTER, SOFTENED
A FEW DROPS OF PINK FOOD COLOURING
2 TEASPOONS STRAWBERRY ESSENCE
1–2 TABLESPOONS WHOLE MILK

TO DECORATE
12 STRAWBERRY LACES
PINK EDIBLE GLITTER
12 SMALL WHOLE STRAWBERRIES
SMARTIES

EQUIPMENT: MIXER, 12-HOLE MUFFIN TIN LINED WITH MUFFIN CASES, PIPING BAG FITTED WITH LARGE STAR NOZZLE

Preheat the oven to 160°C/325°F/Gas Mark 3.

Using a mixer, whisk together the butter and caster sugar until light and creamy. Add the eggs and whisk again. Gently fold in the flour, baking powder, vanilla and a few drops of pink food colouring, using a spatula.

Divide the mixture between the muffin cases and bake for 20 minutes, until the cakes are firm and spring back to your touch. Transfer to a rack to cool.

For the buttercream, whisk together the icing sugar, butter, a few drops of pink food colouring, the strawberry essence and enough milk to make a smooth, stiff frosting. Spoon it into the piping bag and pipe round swirls over the top of each cake. Decorate with a long strand of strawberry lace in a swirled pattern, sprinkle with edible glitter and finish off by topping with a strawberry and some Smarties.

As these cakes are topped with fresh fruit they are best served on the day they are made, although you can store them for up to 3 days in an airtight container if you omit the strawberries.

BEE CAKES

These little buzzy bees with their fondant wings and fizzy cola laces are great for kids' parties. Kids just love them.

PREPARATION TIME: 25 MINUTES

BAKING TIME: 20 MINUTES

MAKES 12 CAKES

FOR THE CUPCAKES

200G UNSALTED BUTTER, SOFTENED

220G CASTER SUGAR

4 EGGS

220G SELF-RAISING FLOUR, SIFTED

2 TEASPOONS BAKING POWDER

4 TABLESPOONS RUNNY HONEY

YELLOW FOOD COLOURING

FOR THE BUTTERCREAM

300G ICING SUGAR, SIFTED

150G UNSALTED BUTTER, SOFTENED

YELLOW FOOD COLOURING

1–2 TABLESPOONS WHOLE MILK

FOR DECORATION

24 WHITE CHOCOLATE BUTTONS

24 BLACK SUGAR PEARL BEADS

STRAWBERRY LACES

WHITE FONDANT

FLAT FIZZY COLA LACES

EQUIPMENT: MIXER, 12-HOLE MUFFIN TIN LINED WITH MUFFIN CASES, SMALL ROUND CUTTER ABOUT 2CM IN DIAMETER

Preheat the oven to 160°C/325°F/Gas Mark 3.

Using a mixer, whisk together the butter and caster sugar until light and creamy. Add the eggs and whisk again. Gently fold in the flour, baking powder and honey, using a spatula. Colour the batter a bright yellow, using a few drops of food colouring.

Divide the mixture between the muffin cases and bake for 20 minutes, until the cakes are firm and spring back to your touch. Transfer to a rack to cool.

For the buttercream, whisk together the icing sugar, butter, a few drops of yellow food colouring and enough milk to make a smooth, stiff frosting. Spread it over the top of each cake.

Fix a black sugar pearl bead on to each white chocolate button, using a little of the icing to secure it, and place a pair of white chocolate button eyes on top of each cupcake. Make a small mouth at one end of the cake using a little piece of strawberry lace. Roll out the white fondant and cut out wings using the round cutter. Pinch the circles at the end and press them into the yellow icing so they stick into place. Cut the cola laces into strips the same width as the cupcakes and place them on top of the cupcakes a small distance apart to make the bee stripes.

These cakes will store for up to 3 days if stored in an airtight container.

SHEEP CAKES

Young kids love farm animals, and these sheep cakes make a great treat to put in kids' going-home bags at parties.

PREPARATION TIME: 25 MINUTES

BAKING TIME: 20 MINUTES

MAKES 12 CAKES

FOR THE CUPCAKES

200G UNSALTED BUTTER, SOFTENED

220G CASTER SUGAR

4 EGGS

220G SELF-RAISING FLOUR, SIFTED

2 TEASPOONS BAKING POWDER

200G WHITE CHOCOLATE CHIPS

FOR THE BUTTERCREAM

300G ICING SUGAR, SIFTED

150G UNSALTED BUTTER, SOFTENED

1-2 TABLESPOONS WHOLE MILK

TO DECORATE

MINI WHITE MARSHMALLOWS

STRAWBERRY LACES

24 WHITE CHOCOLATE BUTTONS

24 SUGAR PEARL BEADS

EQUIPMENT: MIXER, 12-HOLE MUFFIN TIN LINED WITH MUFFIN CASES

Preheat the oven to 160°C/325°F/Gas Mark 3.

Using a mixer, whisk together the butter and caster sugar until light and creamy. Add the eggs and whisk again. Gently fold in the flour, baking powder and white chocolate chips, using a spatula.

Divide the mixture between the muffin cases and bake for 20 minutes, until the cakes are firm and spring back to your touch. Transfer to a rack to cool.

For the icing, whisk together the icing sugar, butter and enough milk to make a smooth, stiff frosting. Spread it over the top of each cake and decorate with a layer of mini marshmallows to look like a sheep's fleece. Add a smile with a small piece of red strawberry lace. Fix a black sugar pearl bead on to each white chocolate button, using a little of the buttercream to secure it, and place a pair of white chocolate button eyes on top of each cupcake.

These cakes will store for up to 3 days in an airtight container.

FROG CAKES

These frog cakes are not the slightest bit slimy, although they are very green. With white chocolate button eyes and red bootlace smiles, they will brighten up any rainy day.

PREPARATION TIME: 25 MINUTES

BAKING TIME: 20 MINUTES

MAKES 12 CAKES

FOR THE CUPCAKES

200G UNSALTED BUTTER, SOFTENED

220G CASTER SUGAR

4 EGGS

220G SELF-RAISING FLOUR, SIFTED

2 TEASPOONS BAKING POWDER

A FEW DROPS OF GREEN FOOD
   COLOURING

FOR THE BUTTERCREAM

300G ICING SUGAR, SIFTED

150G UNSALTED BUTTER, SOFTENED

A FEW DROPS OF GREEN FOOD
   COLOURING

1-2 TABLESPOONS WHOLE MILK

TO DECORATE

24 WHITE CHOCOLATE BUTTONS

24 PEARL BEADS

4 STRAWBERRY LACES

**EQUIPMENT: MIXER, 12-HOLE MUFFIN TIN
LINED WITH MUFFIN CASES**

Preheat the oven to 160°C/325°F Gas Mark 3.

Using a mixer, whisk together the butter and caster sugar until light and creamy. Add the eggs and whisk again. Gently fold in the flour, baking powder and a few drops of green food colouring, using a spatula. You want the batter to be a really vibrant green colour for best effect.

Divide the mixture between the muffin cases and bake for 20 minutes, until the cakes are firm and spring back to your touch. Transfer to a rack to cool.

For the icing, whisk together the icing sugar, butter, a few drops of green food colouring and enough milk to make a smooth, stiff frosting. Spread it over the top of each cake. Use a small amount of the icing to fix pearl beads on to the white chocolate buttons to make the wobbly eyes, then place two eyes on top of each cake. Make a large smile on each cake using the strawberry laces.

These cakes will store for up to 3 days in an airtight container.

RAINBOW PUSH POP CAKES

Push pops are a new fashion that both kids and adults go mad for. They are quick and easy to bake with kids and take no time at all to prepare. My daughter Dixie loves to cut out the circles of cake herself, using a cutter, and her little fingers are perfect for pushing the cake into the tubes. The only help I need to give her is to pipe a swirl of icing between the layers, although older kids would easily be able to do this for themselves. When we are finished, Dixie and I love to decorate our push pops with stickers and ribbons to make them look extra pretty.

You can bake either two or three sponges to use for your push pops, depending on how many colours you want!

Preheat the oven to 160°C/325°F/Gas Mark 3.

Using a mixer, whisk together the butter and caster sugar until light and creamy. Add the eggs and whisk again. Gently fold in the flour, baking powder and vanilla, using a spatula.

Divide the cake mixture between 2 or 3 bowls (depending on how many sponges you are making) and add a few drops of different food colouring to each bowl. Fold in so that each cake batter has an even colour. Spoon one of the cake batters into each cake tin and bake your coloured cakes in the oven for 20 minutes, until they are firm to touch and a skewer inserted into the centre comes out clean, with no cake batter on it. Transfer to a rack to cool.

For the buttercream, whisk together the icing sugar, butter and milk until you have a smooth thick frosting. Divide it equally into separate bowls and add a few drops of different food colouring to each. Whisk each icing well so that it has an even colour. Spoon one of the icings into each piping bag.

Using the cutter, cut out discs of cake. Place a disc in the base of each push pop and pipe a small star of icing on top. Cover with another layer of cake in a different colour and pipe a different coloured swirl of icing. Repeat until the pops are filled with layers of cake and icing in rainbow patterns. Finish with a swirl of icing and decorate with sugar sprinkles. Place the lids on top of the pops and store until you are ready to serve.

PREPARATION TIME: 25 MINUTES
BAKING TIME: 20 MINUTES
MAKES 20 PUSH POPS

FOR THE CAKE MIXTURE
225G UNSALTED BUTTER, SOFTENED
225G CASTER SUGAR
4 EGGS
225G SELF-RAISING FLOUR, SIFTED
2 TEASPOONS BAKING POWDER
1 TEASPOON VANILLA BEAN PASTE
AN ASSORTMENT OF FOOD COLOURINGS
   OF YOUR CHOICE

FOR THE BUTTERCREAM
260G ICING SUGAR, SIFTED
115G UNSALTED BUTTER, SOFTENED
1 TABLESPOON MILK
AN ASSORTMENT OF FOOD COLOURINGS
   OF YOUR CHOICE
1 TEASPOON VANILLA BEAN PASTE

TO DECORATE
RAINBOW SPRINKLES

**EQUIPMENT: 2 OR 3 X 20CM ROUND
SANDWICH CAKE TINS, GREASED AND
LINED, 4CM ROUND CUTTER, 20 PUSH
POPS, 2 OR 3 PIPING BAGS FITTED WITH
LARGE STAR NOZZLES**

Making push pops with Dixie

PERFECT PRINCESS CUPCAKES

Every little girl's dream is to have cupcakes with more pink sparkles and sprinkles than can fit on one cake. These delicate cakes have rainbow sprinkles baked inside them and look magical when they are cut open. If you are short of time you can buy sugar crowns to replace the ones made in the recipe below, or top the cakes with sugar diamonds instead for a real wow factor.

PREPARATION TIME: 25 MINUTES

BAKING TIME: 20 MINUTES

MAKES 12 CAKES

FOR THE CUPCAKES

200G UNSALTED BUTTER, SOFTENED

220G CASTER SUGAR

4 EGGS

220G SELF-RAISING FLOUR, SIFTED

2 TEASPOONS BAKING POWDER

A FEW DROPS OF PINK FOOD COLOURING

6 TABLESPOONS RAINBOW SUGAR
  SPRINKLES

FOR THE CREAM CHEESE FROSTING

450G ICING SUGAR, SIFTED

70G UNSALTED BUTTER, SOFTENED

180G CREAM CHEESE

A FEW DROPS OF PINK FOOD COLOURING

TO DECORATE

200G READY-TO-ROLL FONDANT ICING

GOLD LUSTRE SPRAY

EDIBLE GLITTER

GOLD AND IVORY SUGAR PEARL BEADS

EDIBLE GLUE

**EQUIPMENT: MIXER, 12-HOLE MUFFIN
TIN LINED WITH MUFFIN CASES, PIPING
BAG FITTED WITH LARGE STAR NOZZLE,
CROWN SILICONE MOULD**

Begin by preparing the crown decorations, as they need to dry before being used. Dab the silicone moulds with a little vegetable oil so that the decorations do not stick. Take small pieces of ready-to-roll icing and press them into the moulds so that they take the shape of crowns. Remove from the moulds and place on a silicone mat or a sheet of baking parchment to dry, trimming any excess icing with a sharp knife. Repeat with all the remaining icing. Leave the icing to set for 24 hours. Once the icing is dry, spray with gold lustre spray to decorate. Once dry, decorate the crowns with glitter and sugar pearls, fixing them to the crowns with edible glue.

If you do not have a silicone crown mould, roll out the fondant icing thinly on a surface dusted with icing sugar, into rectangles around 3cm wide and 10cm long. Use a sharp knife to cut diamond shapes along one long edge to make the top of the crown. Pick the crown up and join the two ends with edible glue to make a round shape. Leave to dry, then decorate with gold lustre spray, pearl beads or glitter to bring the crown to life and add some sparkle as above.

Preheat the oven to 160°C/325°F/Gas Mark 3.

Using a mixer, whisk together the butter and caster sugar until light and creamy. Add the eggs and whisk again. Gently fold in the flour, baking powder, pink food colouring and sugar sprinkles, using a spatula, until the batter has an even pink colour.

Divide the mixture between the muffin cases and bake for 20 minutes, until the cakes are firm and spring back to your touch. Transfer to a rack to cool.

For the icing, whisk together the icing sugar, butter and cream cheese in a mixing bowl until light and creamy and add a few drops of pink food colouring. Spoon the icing into a piping bag and pipe pink swirls on top of each cake. Top each one with a decorated crown and add a little more edible glitter for extra sparkle.

CAKE POPS

You can go wild when decorating these pops. They are great for kids' parties, as they can be prepared in advance and stored in the refrigerator until needed. You can add different flavourings to the cake batter too, if you like.

PREPARATION TIME: 30 MINUTES

BAKING TIME: 45–50 MINUTES

MAKES 12–15 POPS

FOR THE CAKE MIXTURE

200G UNSALTED BUTTER, SOFTENED

200G CASTER SUGAR

200G LIGHT BROWN SUGAR

8 EGGS

320G SELF-RAISING FLOUR, SIFTED

120G COCOA POWDER, SIFTED

1 TEASPOON BICARBONATE OF SODA

160ML SOURED CREAM

4 TEASPOONS VANILLA BEAN PASTE

A PINCH OF SALT

FOR THE ICING

300G ICING SUGAR, SIFTED

150G UNSALTED BUTTER, SOFTENED

1-2 TABLESPOONS WHOLE MILK

TO DECORATE

330G CANDY MELTS

SUGAR SPRINKLES OR SUGAR SAND

EQUIPMENT: MIXER, 20CM SQUARE CAKE TIN, GREASED AND LINED, CAKE POP STICKS

Preheat the oven to 160°C/325°F/Gas Mark 3.

Using a mixer, whisk together the butter, caster sugar and light brown sugar until light and creamy. Add the eggs and whisk again. Gently fold in the flour, cocoa powder, bicarbonate of soda, soured cream, vanilla bean paste and salt, using a spatula.

Spoon the mixture into the cake tin and bake for 45–50 minutes, until the cake is firm to touch and a skewer inserted into the centre comes out clean, with no cake batter on it. Transfer to a rack to cool.

For the icing, whisk together the icing sugar, butter and milk.

Once the cake has cooled, put it into a food processor or make it into crumbs with your hands. Mix it with the buttercream to make a mouldable cake mix. Roll the mixture into balls weighing about 35g each. Leave them to set in the fridge overnight (or if you are short of time, you can freeze them for 15 minutes instead).

Melt the candy melts in a heatproof bowl over a saucepan of simmering water. Candy melts can also be melted in the microwave: stir at 20-second intervals until smooth and runny. If they are not as runny as you would like, add 1-2 teaspoons of vegetable oil. Dip each pop stick into the candy melts and stick them into the ends of the cake pops. Leave to set so that the sticks are secure. Once secure, dip the pops into the melt and, before the chocolate sets, decorate with sugar sand or sprinkles.

TREASURE ISLAND CUPCAKES

'Yo ho ho and a bottle of rum!!!' No pirate party is complete without these fantastical cakes topped with treasure chests and gold coins. Boys (and girls too) just adore these.

PREPARATION TIME: 25 MINUTES

BAKING TIME: 20 MINUTES

MAKES 12 CAKES

FOR THE CUPCAKES
200G UNSALTED BUTTER, SOFTENED
220G CASTER SUGAR
4 EGGS
220G SELF-RAISING FLOUR, SIFTED
2 TEASPOONS BAKING POWDER
ZEST OF 2 LEMONS

FOR THE CREAM CHEESE FROSTING
450G ICING SUGAR, SIFTED
70G UNSALTED BUTTER, SOFTENED
180G CREAM CHEESE
YELLOW FOOD COLOURING
4 DIGESTIVE BISCUITS

TO DECORATE
200G READY-TO-ROLL FONDANT ICING
BROWN FOOD COLOURING
GOLD SUGAR SAND
GOLD AND IVORY SUGAR PEARL BEADS
30G GOLDEN MARZIPAN
GOLD CHOCOLATE COINS

EQUIPMENT: MIXER, 12-HOLE MUFFIN TIN LINED WITH MUFFIN CASES, PIPING BAG FITTED WITH STAR NOZZLE

Preheat the oven to 160°C/325°F/Gas Mark 3.

Using a mixer, whisk together the butter and caster sugar until light and creamy. Add the eggs and whisk again. Gently fold in the flour, baking powder and lemon zest, using a spatula.

Spoon the cake mixture into the muffin cases and bake for 20 minutes, until the cakes are firm and spring back to your touch. Transfer to a rack to cool.

For the frosting, whisk together the icing sugar, butter and cream cheese in a mixing bowl until light and creamy. Add a few drops of yellow food colouring and mix again. Pipe it over the top of the cakes. Blitz the digestive biscuits to fine crumbs in a food processor and sprinkle over the icing to look like sand.

For the decorations, colour the fondant icing brown with a little food colouring, kneading it in your hands on a surface dusted with icing sugar until it is an even colour. Make small chest shapes by making rectangles for the bases of the chests around 3cm deep, 3cm wide and 5cm long. Make tops for the chests that are the same size but curved. Using a sharp knife, score wood marks into both the bottoms and tops of the chests to make them look more realistic. Press a dent into the top of each rectangular base and fill this with gold sugar sand and gold and ivory pearl beads.

Roll out the marzipan on a surface dusted with icing sugar and cut out small circles to look like small gold coins, using a small round icing nozzle. Place a treasure chest top on each of the rectangle bases, pressing down lightly on one long side so that it looks like an open trunk containing treasure. Place a chest on top of each cupcake and decorate with chocolate coins as well.

Decorating tip: To make a treasure map, cut a piece of ivory fondant into a square and roll out thinly on a surface dusted with icing sugar. Break the edges to make them look jagged and curl them up to look like an old map. Using an edible ink pen, draw a map on the icing. Leave to dry before putting on top of the cakes. The decorations, and the treasure chests, can be made up to a week in advance.

SKINNY MINNIE CUPCAKES

This chapter contains lower-fat cakes for 'skinny minnies', as I call them, who might not want to overindulge. Smaller portions with low-fat dairy products and reduced sugar means that these cakes can be enjoyed in moderation by those watching their weight.

SKINNY MINNIE LEMON MERINGUE CUPCAKES

Everyone likes a treat once in a while, but on occasion we all try to be well behaved and these low-sugar, low-fat cupcakes are a great option, allowing us to indulge without feeling too naughty. For a really low-sugar alternative, you can serve these cupcakes without any topping for elevenses – the perfect mid-morning guilt-free treat.

PREPARATION TIME: 25 MINUTES

BAKING TIME: 20 MINUTES

MAKES 12 CAKES

FOR THE CUPCAKES

60G LIGHT MARGARINE

225G SUGAR REPLACEMENT, SUCH AS
SPLENDA

115G UNSWEETENED APPLE PURÉE

2 TEASPOONS LEMON ESSENCE

ZEST OF 1 LEMON

185G SELF-RAISING FLOUR, SIFTED

2 TEASPOONS BAKING POWDER

4 EGG WHITES

FOR THE MERINGUE

125G CASTER SUGAR (OR REDUCED-SUGAR
SUBSTITUTE)

2 EGG WHITES

1 TABLESPOON WATER

A PINCH OF SALT

TO ASSEMBLE

2–3 TABLESPOONS LOW-SUGAR LEMON
CURD

**EQUIPMENT: MIXER, 12-HOLE MUFFIN
TIN LINED WITH MUFFIN CASES, SUGAR
THERMOMETER, PIPING BAG FITTED
WITH LARGE STAR NOZZLE, CHEF'S
BLOWTORCH**

Preheat the oven to 170°C/325°F/Gas Mark 3.

Using a mixer, whisk together the margarine and sugar replacement until light and creamy. Mix in the apple purée, lemon essence and zest, flour and baking powder. In a separate bowl, whisk the egg whites to stiff peaks and fold into the cake batter.

Divide the mixture between the muffin cases and bake for 20 minutes, until the cakes are firm and spring back to your touch. Transfer to a rack to cool.

For the meringue, place the caster sugar, egg whites, water and salt in a heatproof bowl over a pan of simmering water. Whisk all the time until the sugar has melted and the mixture reaches 60°C. Remove the bowl from the heat and whisk vigorously until the mixture becomes meringue-like.

Spread a little lemon curd over the top of each cupcake. Spoon the meringue into the piping bag and pipe a large swirl on top of each cake. Use the blowtorch to gently caramelize the meringue until it is golden brown.

Because of the meringue topping, these cakes are best eaten on the day they are made.

ETON MESS CUPCAKES

Eton Mess is one of those great last-minute, chuck-it-all-together desserts - fresh berries, crushed meringue and lots of cream. It's not great for those on a diet, given the high fat content, so why not try these healthier cupcakes for a treat instead?

PREPARATION TIME: 25 MINUTES
BAKING TIME: 20 MINUTES
MAKES 12 CAKES

FOR THE CUPCAKES
200G SELF-RAISING FLOUR, SIFTED
½ TEASPOON SALT
½ TEASPOON BAKING POWDER
¼ TEASPOON BICARBONATE OF SODA
225G SUGAR REPLACEMENT (SUCH AS
   SPLENDA)
110G LOW-FAT MARGARINE
2 EGG WHITES
2 TEASPOONS VANILLA EXTRACT
175G REDUCED-FAT SOURED CREAM
180ML SKIMMED MILK

FOR THE MARSHMALLOW TOPPING
250G CASTER SUGAR
3 EGG WHITES
2 TABLESPOONS COLD WATER
200G STRAWBERRIES, HULLED AND
   CHOPPED

TO DECORATE
MERINGUE PIECES AND MINI
MARSHMALLOWS (OPTIONAL)
BLUEBERRIES (OPTIONAL)

EQUIPMENT: MIXER, 12-HOLE MUFFIN
TIN LINED WITH MUFFIN CASES, SUGAR
THERMOMETER

Preheat the oven to 160°C/325°F/Gas Mark 3.

Stir together the flour, salt, baking powder and bicarbonate of soda in a large bowl. Using a mixer, beat together the sugar replacement and margarine. Beat in the flour mixture, then fold in the egg whites together with the vanilla extract. Add the soured cream and milk and mix so that everything is incorporated. Divide the mixture between the muffin cases and bake for 20 minutes, until the cakes are firm and spring back to your touch. Transfer to a rack to cool.

For the marshmallow topping, place the sugar, egg whites and water in a large saucepan and heat to 60°C, whisking continuously. Once it reaches 60°C, remove it from the heat and pour it into the bowl of a stand mixer with whisk attachment. Whisk until the mixture is stiff and glossy peaks are formed. Fold in the chopped strawberries, then spoon a mound on top of each cake and sprinkle with meringue pieces and mini marshmallows or top with blueberries.

Serve straight away. These cakes are best eaten on the day they are made.

RAINBOW CUPCAKES

These cakes are great as a small treat to brighten up a day when you are dieting.

PREPARATION TIME: 25 MINUTES

BAKING TIME: 20 MINUTES

MAKES 12 CAKES

FOR THE CUPCAKES

200G SELF-RAISING FLOUR, SIFTED

½ TEASPOON SALT

½ TEASPOON BAKING POWDER

¼ TEASPOON BICARBONATE OF SODA

225G SUGAR REPLACEMENT (SUCH AS
   SPLENDA)

110G LOW-FAT MARGARINE

2 EGG WHITES

2 TEASPOONS VANILLA EXTRACT

175G REDUCED-FAT SOURED CREAM

180ML SKIMMED MILK

FOOD COLOURINGS OF YOUR CHOICE

FOR THE ICING

300G ICING SUGAR

150G LOW-FAT MARGARINE

1-2 TABLESPOONS SKIMMED MILK

4 PASTEL FOOD COLOURINGS

TO DECORATE

RAINBOW SPRINKLES (OPTIONAL)

**EQUIPMENT: MIXER, 12-HOLE MUFFIN
TIN LINED WITH MUFFIN CASES, SUGAR
THERMOMETER, PIPING BAG WITH STAR
NOZZLE**

Preheat the oven to 160°C/325°F/Gas Mark 3.

Stir together the flour, salt, baking powder and bicarbonate of soda in a large bowl. Using a mixer, beat together the sugar replacement and margarine. Beat in the flour mix, then fold in the egg whites, together with the vanilla. Add the soured cream and milk and mix so that everything is incorporated.

Divide the mixture between 4 bowls and colour each batch with a few drops of food colouring so that you have four brightly coloured batters. Layer the different coloured batters into the muffin cases until two-thirds full, then bake for 20 minutes, until the cakes are firm and spring back to your touch. Transfer to a rack to cool.

For the icing, whisk together the icing sugar, margarine and enough milk to make a smooth, stiff frosting. Divide the mixture between four bowls and colour each batch a different shade. Spoon the different coloured icings into the piping bag so they are side by side, rather than one on top of the other. Pipe onto each cake for a gorgeous rainbow effect.

These cakes are best eaten on the day they are made.

SKINNY CARROT CUPCAKES

These carrot cakes topped with cream cheese frosting are one of my favourites. You can add chopped walnuts to the cake batter if you like, for extra crunch.

PREPARATION TIME: 25 MINUTES
BAKING TIME: 20 MINUTES
MAKES 12 CAKES

FOR THE CUPCAKES
320G SELF-RAISING FLOUR, SIFTED
2 TEASPOONS BAKING POWDER
1 TEASPOON GROUND CINNAMON
A PINCH OF FRESHLY GRATED NUTMEG
260G LOW-FAT MARGARINE
260G SOFT BROWN SUGAR
160G GRATED CARROT
4 EGGS

FOR THE CREAM CHEESE FROSTING
450G ICING SUGAR, SIFTED
70G UNSALTED BUTTER, SOFTENED
180G LOW-FAT CREAM CHEESE
ZEST AND JUICE OF 1 ORANGE

TO DECORATE
GROUND CINNAMON, FOR DUSTING
CANDIED CARROT PEEL (OPTIONAL)

**EQUIPMENT: MIXER, 12-HOLE MUFFIN TIN
LINED WITH MUFFIN CASES, PIPING BAG
FITTED WITH LARGE ROUND NOZZLE**

Preheat the oven to 160°C/325°F/Gas Mark 3.

Using a mixer, whisk all the cake ingredients together until creamy. Divide the mixture between the muffin cases and bake for 20 minutes, until the cakes are firm and spring back to your touch. Transfer to a rack to cool.

For the frosting, whisk together the icing sugar, butter, cream cheese, orange juice and zest in a mixing bowl until light and creamy. Spoon into the piping bag and pipe a swirl on top of the cooled cupcakes. Dust the cakes with a little ground cinnamon and decorate with candied carrot peel if you like.

The cakes will keep for up to 3 days in an airtight container.

SKINNY VELVET CUPCAKES

Red Velvet cakes have recently become popular in Britain, but they have been a favourite in America for a long time. These are my skinny versions of these fab cocoa-inspired cupcakes. If you are really watching the calories, you can serve these cakes without any icing, or replace the frosting with a drizzle of melted high-cocoa-content plain chocolate instead.

PREPARATION TIME: 25 MINUTES

BAKING TIME: 20 MINUTES

MAKES 12 CAKES

FOR THE CUPCAKES

225G SELF-RAISING FLOUR, SIFTED

150G WHOLEMEAL FLOUR, SIFTED

1 TEASPOON SALT

30G COCOA POWDER

1 TEASPOON BAKING POWDER

225G SUGAR REPLACEMENT

110G UNSWEETENED APPLE PURÉE

56G LOW-FAT MARGARINE

1 WHOLE EGG AND 2 EGG WHITES

2 TEASPOONS VANILLA BEAN PASTE OR
VANILLA EXTRACT

1 TEASPOON BICARBONATE OF SODA

1½ TEASPOONS WHITE VINEGAR

400G BUTTERMILK

1½ TABLESPOONS RED FOOD COLOURING

FOR THE CREAM CHEESE FROSTING

450G ICING SUGAR, SIFTED

70G UNSALTED BUTTER, SOFTENED

180G LOW-FAT CREAM CHEESE

TO DECORATE

COCOA POWDER, FOR DUSTING

**EQUIPMENT: MIXER, 12-HOLE MUFFIN TIN
LINED WITH MUFFIN CASES, PIPING BAG
FITTED WITH LARGE ROUND NOZZLE**

Preheat the oven to 160°C/325°F/Gas Mark 3.

Stir together the flours, salt, cocoa powder and baking powder in a large bowl. Using a mixer, beat together the sugar replacement, apple purée and margarine. Beat in the whole egg and the egg whites, together with the vanilla. In a separate bowl, mix the bicarbonate of soda and vinegar together.

Add half the dry ingredients to the egg mixture and mix well. Add the buttermilk and the red food colouring and mix well. Add the remaining dry ingredients, then fold in the vinegar mixture until everything is incorporated. Divide the mixture between the cake cases and bake for 20 minutes, until the cakes are firm and spring back to your touch. Transfer to a rack to cool.

For the icing, whisk together the icing sugar, butter and cream cheese in a mixing bowl until light and creamy. Spoon into the piping bag and pipe a swirl on top of the cooled cupcakes. Dust the cakes with a little cocoa powder before serving.

The cakes will store for up to 3 days in an airtight container.

QUIRKY CUPCAKES

My passion for baking can sometimes take me down a crazy path and although occasionally they are a little too quirky, the recipes in this chapter are the ones that work. The flavours may sound odd but you have to trust me – they are delicious!

CHOCOLATE CREAM EGG CUPCAKES

These are one of my best-selling cupcakes at Easter. People love the gooey eggs splattered on top of the cakes. The hidden eggs in the centre melt when the cakes are returned to the oven, and these make a great surprise when people bite into them. I like to use Cadbury Mini Creme Eggs for my cakes.

PREPARATION TIME: 25 MINUTES
BAKING TIME: 20 MINUTES
MAKES 12 CAKES

FOR THE CUPCAKES
100G UNSALTED BUTTER, SOFTENED
100G CASTER SUGAR
100G LIGHT BROWN SUGAR
4 EGGS
160G SELF-RAISING FLOUR, SIFTED
60G COCOA POWDER, SIFTED
1 TEASPOON BICARBONATE OF SODA
80ML SOURED CREAM
2 TEASPOONS VANILLA BEAN PASTE
A PINCH OF SALT
12 MINI MILK CHOCOLATE FONDANT EGGS

FOR THE BUTTERCREAM
300G ICING SUGAR, SIFTED
40G COCOA POWDER, SIFTED
150G UNSALTED BUTTER, SOFTENED
60ML MILK

TO DECORATE
200G ICING SUGAR
YELLOW FOOD COLOURING
12 MINI MILK CHOCOLATE FONDANT EGGS

EQUIPMENT: MIXER, 12-HOLE MUFFIN TIN LINED WITH MUFFIN CASES, CUPCAKE PLUNGER OR SHARP KNIFE, PIPING BAG FITTED WITH STAR NOZZLE

Preheat the oven to 160°C/325°F/Gas Mark 3.

Using a mixer, whisk together the butter, caster sugar and light brown sugar until light and creamy. Add the eggs and whisk again. Gently fold in the flour, cocoa powder and bicarbonate of soda, soured cream, vanilla bean paste and salt, using a spatula.

Divide the cake mixture between the muffin cases and bake for 20 minutes, until the cakes are almost firm to touch. Remove from the oven and leave to cool for 10 minutes. When the cakes are cool enough to handle, cut out the centre of each one using the cupcake plunger or a sharp knife. Unwrap the mini chocolate eggs and place one into each hole in the cupcakes, then place the removed cake back on top. Return the cakes to the oven and cook for about a further 2 minutes, until the eggs have melted. Transfer to a rack to cool.

For the buttercream, whisk together the icing sugar, cocoa powder, butter and milk to make a rich chocolate frosting. Pipe a thick layer over the top of each cake. Mix the icing sugar for the decoration with about 1–2 tablespoons of water until smooth and thick. Divide the icing between 2 bowls and colour one batch with a few drops of yellow food colour, mixing until the colouring is an evenly bright yellow.

Spoon a little white icing on top of each cake and top with a little yellow icing. Unwrap the remaining mini eggs and cut each one in half. Place two egg halves on top of the white and yellow icing so that it looks as if the egg has been cracked on top of the cake.

The cakes will keep for up to 3 days if stored in an airtight container.

COLA CUPCAKES

Fizzy cola bottles were one of my favourite sweets as a kid, and Dixie loves them too (although I try not to give them to her too often!). These are great cakes to serve for kids' parties - cola and chocolate are a match made in heaven.

PREPARATION TIME: 25 MINUTES

BAKING TIME: 20 MINUTES

MAKES 12 CAKES

FOR THE CUPCAKES

200G UNSALTED BUTTER, SOFTENED

220G CASTER SUGAR

4 EGGS

420G SELF-RAISING FLOUR, SIFTED

2 TEASPOONS BAKING POWDER

2 TEASPOONS VANILLA BEAN PASTE OR
   VANILLA EXTRACT

400ML COLA

4 TABLESPOONS COCOA POWDER, SIFTED

200ML MILK

FOR THE BUTTERCREAM

300G ICING SUGAR, SIFTED

30G COCOA POWDER, SIFTED

150G UNSALTED BUTTER

EITHER 50ML COLA OR 1½ TABLESPOONS
   COLA EXTRACT

TO DECORATE

FIZZY COLA BOTTLES

**EQUIPMENT: MIXER, 12-HOLE MUFFIN TIN
LINED WITH MUFFIN CASES, PIPING BAG
FITTED WITH STAR NOZZLE**

Preheat the oven to 160°C/325°F/Gas Mark 3.

Using a mixer, whisk together the butter and caster sugar until light and creamy. Add the eggs and whisk again. Gently fold in the flour, baking powder, vanilla bean paste, cola, cocoa powder and milk, using a spatula.

Spoon the cake mixture into the muffin cases. Bake for 20 minutes, until the cakes are firm and spring back to your touch. Transfer to a rack to cool.

For the buttercream, whisk together the icing sugar, cocoa powder, butter and cola or cola extract to make a smooth, stiff frosting. If your icing is a little too runny after adding the cola, just add 50-70g icing sugar a little at a time and mix after each addition until you get the desired consistency. Pipe it over the top of each cake and decorate with fizzy cola bottles.

The cakes will keep for up to 3 days if stored in an airtight container.

COURGETTE CUPCAKES

Although it may seem very quirky to make a sweet cake with courgettes in it, the courgette itself has no flavour and just gives the cupcakes a wonderfully moist texture. With hints of lemon and lime, these little cakes are really refreshing, particularly when topped with a rich cream cheese frosting.

PREPARATION TIME: 25 MINUTES
BAKING TIME: 20 MINUTES
MAKES 12 CAKES

FOR THE CUPCAKES
200G UNSALTED BUTTER, SOFTENED
220G CASTER SUGAR
4 EGGS
220G SELF-RAISING FLOUR, SIFTED
2 TEASPOONS BAKING POWDER
240G COURGETTES, ENDS TRIMMED,
   COARSELY GRATED
ZEST AND JUICE OF 4 LEMONS

FOR THE CREAM CHEESE ICING
450G ICING SUGAR, SIFTED
70G UNSALTED BUTTER, SOFTENED
180G CREAM CHEESE
JUICE AND ZEST OF 2 LIMES

EQUIPMENT: MIXER, GRATER, 12-HOLE MUFFIN TIN LINED WITH MUFFIN CASES, PIPING BAG FITTED WITH A ROUND NOZZLE

Preheat the oven to 160°C/325°F/Gas Mark 3.

Using a mixer, whisk together the butter and caster sugar until light and creamy. Add the eggs and whisk again. Gently fold in the flour, baking powder, grated courgette and the lemon juice and zest, using a spatula.

Divide the mixture between the muffin cases and bake for 20 minutes, until the cakes are firm and spring back to your touch. Transfer to a rack to cool.

For the icing, whisk together the icing sugar, butter, cream cheese and the lime juice and zest in a mixing bowl until light and creamy. Spoon into the piping bag and pipe a swirl on top of each cooled cupcake.

The cakes will keep for up to 3 days if stored in an airtight container.

LOVE ME, HATE ME CUPCAKES

When I appeared on the BBC's The Apprentice, I was one of those love-me or hate-me contestants, just like Marmite! To celebrate my appearance we made these cakes in the shop - you will have to trust me that this combination does actually taste good, although if you are not convinced you can just omit the yeast extract from the recipe and make chocolate cream cheese cupcakes instead! I love to use glossy black muffin cases to show these cakes off to best effect.

PREPARATION TIME: 25 MINUTES

BAKING TIME: 20 MINUTES

MAKES 12 CAKES

FOR THE CUPCAKES

230G UNSALTED BUTTER, SOFTENED

230G CASTER SUGAR

4 EGGS

230G SELF-RAISING FLOUR, SIFTED

60G COCOA POWDER, SIFTED

2 TEASPOONS BAKING POWDER

4 TEASPOONS MARMITE, OR OTHER
    YEAST EXTRACT, DISSOLVED IN 50ML
    HOT WATER

FOR THE BUTTERCREAM

255G ICING SUGAR, SIFTED

30G UNSALTED BUTTER, SOFTENED

60G CREAM CHEESE

1 TABLESPOON MILK

A FEW DROPS OF YELLOW FOOD
    COLOURING

TO DECORATE

CHOCOLATE SPRINKLES

**EQUIPMENT: MIXER, 12-HOLE MUFFIN TIN
LINED WITH BLACK MUFFIN CASES, PIPING
BAG FITTED WITH LARGE ROUND NOZZLE**

Preheat the oven to 160°C/325°F/Gas Mark 3.

Using a mixer, whisk together the butter and caster sugar until light and creamy. Add the eggs and whisk again. Fold in the flour, cocoa powder and baking powder using a spatula, together with the yeast extract liquid. Divide the cake mixture between the muffin cases and bake for 20 minutes, until the cakes are firm and spring back to your touch. Transfer to a rack to cool.

For the buttercream, whisk together the icing sugar, butter, cream cheese, milk and food colouring to make a bright yellow frosting. Spoon into the piping bag and pipe a large swirl on each cooled cake. Decorate with chocolate sprinkles.

The cakes will keep for up to 3 days if stored in an airtight container.

CHOCOLATE GUINNESS® CUPCAKES

These dark cupcakes are dense, moist and chocolatey with the subtle hint of Guinness as a delicious undertone. They're a definite favourite and a must-have for St Patrick's Day celebrations. Decorate them with green glitter and icing or even little sugar shamrocks.

PREPARATION TIME: 30 MINUTES
BAKING TIME: 20 MINUTES
MAKES 12 CAKES

FOR THE CUPCAKES
250ML GUINNESS, OR OTHER STOUT
100G UNSALTED BUTTER, SOFTENED
100G CASTER SUGAR
100G LIGHT BROWN SUGAR
60G COCOA POWDER, SIFTED
4 EGGS
160G SELF-RAISING FLOUR, SIFTED
1 TEASPOON BICARBONATE OF SODA
80ML SOURED CREAM
2 TEASPOONS VANILLA BEAN PASTE
PINCH OF SALT

FOR THE CREAM CHEESE ICING
450G ICING SUGAR, SIFTED
70G UNSALTED BUTTER, SOFTENED
180G CREAM CHEESE

TO DECORATE
GREEN FOOD COLOURING
GREEN GLITTER / SUGAR SAND
GREEN SUGAR SHAMROCKS
  (AVAILABLE ONLINE)

EQUIPMENT: MIXER, 12 HOLE MUFFIN TIN LINED WITH MUFFIN CASES, PIPING BAG FITTED WITH LARGE STAR NOZZLE

Preheat the oven to 160°C/325°F/Gas Mark 3.

Start by pouring the stout into a large, wide saucepan and add the butter; heat until the butter's melted.

Transfer the stout mixture to a mixer, add both sugars and cocoa powder and mix until well combined and creamy. Add the eggs and whisk again. Mix in the flour and bicarbonate of soda, soured cream, vanilla bean paste and salt. Continue to mix until all ingredients are combined and the batter has a smooth texture.

Divide the cake mixture between the cake cases and bake for 20 minutes until the cakes are firm to touch and a knife comes out clean with no cake batter on when inserted into the centre of one of the cakes. Transfer to a rack to cool.

For the icing, in a mixing bowl whisk together the icing sugar, butter and cream cheese until light and creamy. Add a few drops of green food colouring to make it a pale St Patrick's green. Spoon the icing into a piping bag and pipe on top of the cooled cupcakes.

To decorate, sprinkle over some edible glitter, sugar sand, or you could even use some green sugar shamrocks.

The cakes will keep for up to 3 days if stored in an airtight container.

CHOCOLATE JALAPEÑO CUPCAKES

People always look at me like I am a little bit crazy when I serve these cakes. For the really daring, give extra kick to the cake batter by adding finely chopped fresh red chilli too. The red glitter chillies on top always prove to be a good talking point – eat them only if you are brave enough! You can buy the chilli syrup online, from specialist suppliers, or make your own by steeping chillies in sugar syrup.

PREPARATION TIME: 25 MINUTES

BAKING TIME: 20 MINUTES

MAKES 12 CAKES

FOR THE CUPCAKES
100G UNSALTED BUTTER, SOFTENED
100G CASTER SUGAR
100G LIGHT BROWN SUGAR
4 EGGS
160G SELF-RAISING FLOUR, SIFTED
60G COCOA POWDER, SIFTED
1 TEASPOON BICARBONATE OF SODA
80ML SOURED CREAM
2 TEASPOONS VANILLA BEAN PASTE
4 TEASPOONS CAYENNE PEPPER
2 TABLESPOONS CHILLI SYRUP
A PINCH OF SALT
1–2 FINELY CHOPPED RED CHILLIES
    (OPTIONAL)

FOR THE BUTTERCREAM
300G ICING SUGAR, SIFTED
40G COCOA POWDER, SIFTED
150G UNSALTED BUTTER, SOFTENED
60ML MILK
1 TEASPOON CHILLI SYRUP

TO DECORATE
12 WHOLE CHILLIES
EDIBLE GLUE
RED EDIBLE GLITTER

**EQUIPMENT: MIXER, 12-HOLE MUFFIN TIN
LINED WITH MUFFIN CASES, PIPING BAG
WITH STAR NOZZLE**

Preheat the oven to 160°C/325°F/Gas Mark 3.

Using a mixer, whisk together the butter, caster sugar and light brown sugar until light and creamy. Add the eggs and whisk again. Fold in the flour, cocoa powder, bicarbonate of soda, soured cream, vanilla bean paste, cayenne pepper, chilli syrup, salt and finely chopped red chilli, if using.

Divide the cake mixture between the muffin cases and bake for 20 minutes, until the cakes are firm and spring back to your touch. Transfer to a rack to cool.

For the icing, whisk together the icing sugar, cocoa powder, butter, milk and chilli syrup to make a rich chocolate frosting. Pipe in a swirl over the top of each cake.

For the decoration, brush the chillies with edible glue and sprinkle them with edible glitter to make them sparkle before putting them on top of the cakes.

The cakes will keep for up to 3 days if stored in an airtight container.

About the Author

Luisa Zissman rose to fame in 2013 when she won a place in the final of *The Apprentice*. She is the founder of three successful businesses: her cupcake company, Dixie's Cupcakery, The Baker Shop, an international online retailer, and Bakers Toolkit. Luisa lives in Hertfordshire with her daughter, Dixie.

Acknowledgements

Vickie White, my manager, who has put up with lots from me! Thanks for your loyalty and support. Daisy, who makes me laugh every day. Michelle and the whole team at Transworld: thank you for believing in this book, it's always been a dream of mine and you have made it come true. Laura, my best friend, who delivered hundreds of cupcakes with me to people one crazy day in London to try and bring this to life. Oliver, for helping build the baking empire! Hollie and my team at work whose dedication never ceases to amaze me. Robin & Gemma for creating such wonderful pictures, Sarah Whittaker for her beautiful design work on the book; and Michelle, thank you for all your help in all aspects of my life!

You can find my baking supplies and cupcakes online at the following:

www.the-bakershop.co.uk
www.bakerstoolkit.co.uk
www.dixiescupcakery.co.uk

And follow us on Twitter!
@bakers_toolkit
@thebakershop
@dixiescupcakery

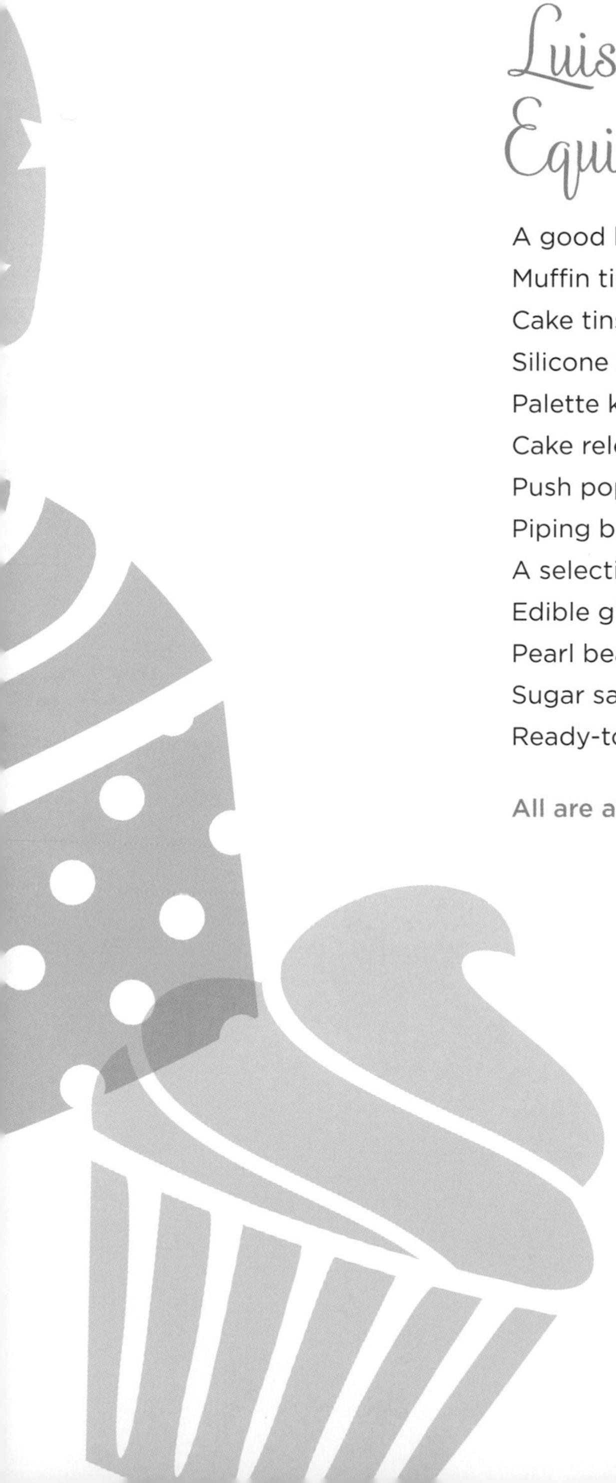

Luisa's Essential Equipment List

A good kitchen mixer – I use KitchenAid

Muffin tin

Cake tins

Silicone moulds

Palette knife

Cake release

Push pop holders

Piping bags

A selection of nozzles

Edible glitter

Pearl beads

Sugar sand

Ready-to-roll icing

All are available to order online from The Baker Shop

INDEX

A

Alice in Wonderland 'Eat Me'
    cupcakes 75
almonds
    almond buttercream 77
    Bakewell tart cupcakes 77
animal cakes
    bee cakes 93
    frog cakes 97
    sheep cakes 94
apples
    apple crumble cupcakes 39
    skinny minnie lemon meringue
        cupcakes 111
    skinny velvet cupcakes 119

B

Bakewell tart cupcakes 77
bee cakes 93
berries
    cheesecake cupcakes 35
    pink champagne cupcakes 44
biscuits
    cheesecake cupcakes 35
    cookies and cream cupcakes 32
buttercream 20–3
    almond 77
    chilli chocolate 133
    chocolate 35, 63–5, 73, 124
    chocolate cream egg 123
    cinnamon frosting 39
    coconut cream cheese 51
    cream cheese 35, 102, 106–7, 127,
        129, 131
    cucumber 52–3

flavouring 20
honey 86–7
lemon 75
mint 52–3
orange 52–3
peanut butter 36
pink champagne cupcakes 44
salted caramel 40
strawberry 52–3, 72, 91
tequila 46
vanilla 73
buttermilk: skinny velvet cupcakes
    119

C

cake cases 16
cake mix 12
cake pops 104
caramel: salted caramel cupcakes
    40
carrots: skinny carrot cupcakes 117
champagne cupcakes 44
cheesecake cupcakes 35
cherries: Bakewell tart cupcakes 77
children's cupcakes 88–107
chillies: chocolate jalapeño
    cupcakes 133
chocolate
    cake pops 104
    chocolate buttercream 30, 63,
        73, 123
    chocolate cream egg cupcakes
        123
    chocolate fondue cupcakes 49
    chocolate Guinness cupcakes 131

chocolate jalapeño cupcakes 133
chocolate mini milk cakes 73
chocolate peanut butter fudge
    cupcakes 36
cola cupcakes 124
hen party cupcakes 63–5
high hats cupcakes 82–5
indulgent chocolate cupcakes 30
love me, hate me cupcakes 14,
    129
sheep cakes 94
skinny velvet cupcakes 119
sugar heart Valentine cupcakes
    61
cinnamon 14
    apple crumble cupcakes 39
CMC powder 22
cola cupcakes 124
coconut: pina colada cupcakes 51
cookies and cream cupcakes 32
courgette cupcakes 127
cream
    chocolate mini milk cakes 73
    strawberry mini milk cakes 72
    vanilla mini milk cakes 73
cream cheese
    cheesecake cupcakes 35
    cream cheese frosting 35, 102,
        106–7, 117, 119, 127, 129, 131
    pina colada cupcakes 51
cream egg cupcakes 123
crème Chantilly 54
cucumber buttercream 52–3
cupcake mix 12

D

daiquiri: strawberry daiquiri cupcakes 54

decorations, hand-made 22

disasters, dealing with 16

dulce de leche: salted caramel cupcakes 40

E

eggs

marshmallow topping 61, 82, 113, 114

skinny minnie lemon meringue cupcakes 111

Eton mess cupcakes 113

F

flavourings 14

buttercream 20

flower paste 22

fondant icing 22, 81

fondue cupcakes, chocolate 49

frog cakes 97

frostings see icing

fudge: chocolate peanut butter fudge cupcakes 36

G

ginger: Pimm's layer cake 52–3

glitter, edible 21

greasing tins 15

Guinness: chocolate Guinness cupcakes 131

H

hen party cupcakes 63–5

high hats cupcakes 82–5

honey

bee cakes 93

honey buttercream 86–7

I

ice cream cone cakes 69

icing

almond buttercream 77

buttercream, tips on working with 20–3

chilli chocolate buttercream 133

chocolate buttercream 30, 63, 73, 123

chocolate cream egg 123

cinnamon frosting 39

coconut cream cheese 51

cream cheese frosting 35, 102, 106–7, 117, 119, 127, 129, 131

crème Chantilly 54

filling icing bags 20

honey buttercream 86–7

lemon buttercream 75

marshmallow topping 61, 82, 113, 114

mint buttercream 52–3

orange buttercream 52–3

peanut butter buttercream 36

piping roses 21

problems with 16

salted caramel buttercream 40

strawberry buttercream 52–3, 72, 91

tequila buttercream 46

vanilla buttercream 73

icing bags 20

indulgent chocolate cupcakes 30

J

jalapeño cupcakes, chocolate 133

jelly shot cupcakes 46

L

lavender button cupcakes 86–7

layer cake, Pimm's 52–3

lemons

Alice in Wonderland 'Eat Me' cupcakes 75

courgette cupcakes 127

lemon buttercream 75

skinny minnie lemon meringue cupcakes 111

treasure island cupcakes 106–7

limes

cream cheese icing 127

jelly shot cupcakes 46

strawberry daiquiri cupcakes 54

lining tins 15

lipstick and lips cupcakes 59

love me, hate me cupcakes 129

M

Malibu: pina colada cupcakes 51

Marmite: love me, hate me cupcakes 14, 129

marshmallow topping 61, 82, 113, 114

meringues: skinny minnie lemon meringue cupcakes 111
Mexican modelling paste 22
milkshake cupcakes 72–3
mint buttercream 52–3

N
nuts
  almond buttercream 77
  Bakewell tart cupcakes 77
  chocolate peanut butter fudge cupcakes 36

O
oranges
  cream cheese frosting 117
  orange buttercream 52–3
Oreo cookies and cream cupcakes 32

P
peanut butter: chocolate peanut butter fudge cupcakes 36
pearls and brooches cupcakes 81
perfect princess cupcakes 102
Pimm's layer cake 52–3
pina colada cupcakes 51
pineapple: pina colada cupcakes 51
pink champagne cupcakes 44
pink heart Valentine cupcakes 61
princess cupcakes 102
push pop cakes, rainbow 98–101

R
rainbow cupcakes 114

rainbow push pop cakes 98–101
raspberry essence: sugar heart Valentine cupcakes 61
raspberry jam: Bakewell tart cupcakes 77
rose water: pearls and brooches cupcakes 81
roses, piping buttercream 21
rum 14

S
salted caramel cupcakes 40
sheep cakes 94
skinny minnie lemon meringue cupcakes 111
skinny carrot cupcakes 117
skinny velvet cupcakes 119
soured cream
  cake pops 104
  chocolate Guinness cupcakes 131
  chocolate jalapeño cupcakes 133
  chocolate peanut butter fudge cupcakes 36
  cream egg cupcakes 123
  Eton mess cupcakes 113
  hen party cupcakes 63–5
  high hats cupcakes 82
  rainbow cupcakes 114
  sugar heart Valentine cupcakes 61
strawberries
  Eton mess cupcakes 113
  pink champagne cupcakes 44
  strawberry buttercream 52–3, 72, 91

strawberry cupcakes 91
strawberry daiquiri cupcakes 54
strawberry mini milk cakes 72
sugar heart Valentine cupcakes 61

T
tequila: jelly shot cupcakes 46
tins, preparing 15
torso and corset cakes 62
treasure island cupcakes 106–7

V
vanilla
  vanilla buttercream 73
  vanilla cupcakes 14
  vanilla mini milk cakes 73
velvet cupcakes, skinny 119